Schooling Homeless Children

A Working Model for America's Public Schools

Schooling Homeless Children

A Working Model for America's Public Schools

Sharon Quint

FOREWORD BY
James P. Comer &
Norris M. Haynes

TEACHERS COLLEGE PRESS

Teachers College, Columbia University
New York and London

All author's royalties from the sale of this book are being
donated to the B. F. Day Foundation for Homeless Children

Published by Teachers College Press, 1234 Amsterdam Avenue, New York, N.Y. 10027

Copyright © 1994 by Teachers College, Columbia University

Photographs pp. 2 & 82 Copyright ©1993 *Seattle Times*. Used with permission.
Photographs pp. 19 & 74 used by permission of *Education Week*.
All other photographs by John McAlvey and Don Zemke.

Library of Congress Cataloging-in-Publication Data

Quint, Sharon, date.
   Schooling homeless children : working model for America's public
schools / Sharon Quint.
     p.   cm.
   Includes bibliographical references (p.) and index.
   ISBN 0-8077-3392-X (alk. paper).—ISBN 0-8077-3391-1 (pbk. :
alk. paper)
   1. Homeless children—Education (Elementary)—Washington—Seattle—
Case studies. 2. Benjamin Franklin Day Elementary School (Seattle,
Wash.) I. Title.
   LC5144.22.W2Q85   1994
   371.96´7´09797772—dc20   94-28783

ISBN 0-8077-3391-1 (paper)
ISBN 0-8077-3392-x (cloth)   BK
                      $17.95

Printed on acid-free paper
Manufactured in the United States of America
07 06   8 7 6 5 4

Dedication

To my mother, Celia, the heart of our family
whose love and good nature know no bounds

To my father, Harry, a wise and noble man
whose memory continues to inspire me

To my daughter, Lauren, who always asks,
"Why does it have to be this way?"

To my son, Ricky, who always responds,
"What if it were different?"

And to my best friend, my husband, Jay,
who has taught me that love conquers all pain.

Never doubt that a small group of thoughtful and committed citizens can change the world. Indeed, it is the only thing that ever does.

—*Margaret Mead*

Contents

Foreword

The problems that plague our nation's schools are manifold, and most of us are painfully aware of the continuing debate about their toll on the millions of school children in this country. However, the issue of homelessness in schools is one that, despite it's prevalence, has only recently been recognized, and minimally addressed. Sharon Quint's *Schooling Homeless Children* takes on this issue with compassion, and will undoubtedly have an effect on future reform efforts to improve the schooling of our children.

The remarkable story of the Benjamin Franklin Day Elementary School in Seattle, Washington, is vividly conveyed by Dr. Quint. In her preface, the author shares with us how her own personal experience has fueled her commitment to advocate for children who are often forced into terrifying niches in society, where their cries are not heard. She quite wonderfully recounts the vigor and struggle of the teachers, students, and staff of this school in the chapters that follow. The depth and strength of Dr. Quint's commitment is reflected in the passion with which she tells the important story of the school's transformation into a social as well as educational institution.

One cannot read this book without gaining deep admiration for Carole Williams, the principal of "B. F. Day." Williams deserves praise for her personal struggle to better the lives of the children in her school by boldly redefining the traditional role of a school principal. The energy and undying commitment with which she confronted this challenge sent a powerful pulse throughout the school, which resonated not only with teachers and staff, but with parents and community leaders as well.

But most importantly this story is about the children of B. F. Day. As Dr. Quint reminds us, we can hardly expect a child who has spent the night in a chaotic shelter, or on a cold and unyielding park bench, to come to school eager and ready to learn. Beginning from this premise— that children cannot learn when they are tired, hungry, and/or worried about where they will be sleeping each night—Carole Williams and her staff made special efforts to meet the needs of the many homeless children at B. F. Day. By inspiring and empowering everyone around her, Williams successfully created a school climate that fostered a crucial sense of belongingness for all of the children. A small but wonderful example is her creation of a "transition room," where the children could "unload" all of their negative and painful feelings in the presence of a caring and supportive adult. Especially for those children identified as homeless, this room became important as a buffer against the disorienting and dissociative effects of their difficult and unpredictable lives outside of school.

Williams also challenged teachers to step outside the school building into the harsh environments in which the children lived. By actively exploring the community, teachers and staff at B. F. Day could begin to see the world from the children's perspective, to comprehend the often perilous nature of their home and neighborhood environments. They joined with the children both inside and outside of the school walls, thus bridging the gap that marginalizes so many of our nation's schools.

In sum, the grassroots effort at B. F. Day embraces all of the necessary components for effecting positive changes in our nation's schools. The principal's dynamic leadership strengthened ties between teachers, inspired them, and reaffirmed their commitment to helping children. Community coalitions were developed to secure financial and social support. All of these changes emphasized the importance of global school change and fostered a school climate in which everyone could feel safe and cared for. Dr. Quint paints an inspiring and realistic picture of this process.

James P. Comer and Norris M. Haynes
Yale Child Study Center

Preface

The "street kids," as they were often referred to in the 1950s, were as much a part of my early childhood as ice cream sodas, sore throats, and homework. They skipped barefoot and free in the summers, running jubilantly through the cool rain of an after-dark thunderstorm. They jumped fearlessly onto the backs of city buses for a two- or three-block joy ride and then flaunted their bruises and abrasions as if they were badges of courage. Their ragged clothes, smudged faces, and tangled hair reflected a freedom from parental restrictions that I secretly longed for.

Often the street kids rummaged through trash cans parked just along the curb outside Nathan's-the best hot dog place in the whole world. On a Saturday afternoon, they were sure to find pretty good-sized portions of french fries, watermelon slices, and hamburgers. A half-eaten hot dog was a rare find because people just couldn't resist finishing a Nathan's frankfurter down to the last bite. I wasn't allowed to eat food found in the garbage, but I was allowed to play with the street kids.

My family moved to the Coney Island Projects—only 20 blocks from Nathan's—when I was 5 years old. Before that we lived in a five-flight walk-up on the Lower East Side. My parents often talked about the move as "a step upward" because the projects were brand new, had an elevator, and didn't have mice or roaches. Anyway, the clean ocean air and the amusement rides were a far better environment for growing teenagers like my sister and brother, or so my dad often said. My father was a public school teacher. Sometimes he taught in the high school and sometimes in the elementary school. In the evenings, he taught English classes to the foreign-born.

If I was lucky enough to tag along with my dad, the hours just after school on Tuesdays and Thursdays were the most adventurous. We would walk up Surf Avenue, then skirt along Mermaid until we reached Neptune and the bay. As we walked, my dad would approach the street kids, whom he seemed to know by first name. The kids would scream with glee, "The teacher! The teacher!" Sometimes the kids would just run up to my father and start swinging his hand. Often, he would hug them or pat them on the shoulder and then say things like, "You weren't in class today, so I'll assume there was a problem. I expect to see you tomorrow" or "You didn't behave nicely in class today. Come sit on the curb with me and let's talk about what's troubling you." On Mondays and Wednesdays, my dad brought the street kids home with him in order to "teach them their letter and number facts so the grocer and the butcher couldn't cheat them."

Sometimes he would read stories to all of us about far-away places like Central Park, Radio City Music Hall, or the Bronx Zoo "because the world is bigger than Coney Island and everyone has to be ready to take a step upward."

I remember my dad best when he held me close to his heart and whispered, "I love you more than the whole wide world. You are my little angel, a gift from God." He would talk in a sad voice about "the stupidity of prejudice against the Negroes and the Jews" and about "the street kids trapped in poverty with no way out." He would think out loud about finding ways to get the street kids warm coats and shoes for the winter. Once he had my mother take down the drapes in the living room and sew six jackets for "the Negro family living in an abandoned building on Mermaid and 32nd Street." Many times, he cut up old rubber tires and glued pieces to the bottom of worn shoes. We unraveled the wool from old sweaters so my mom could knit mittens for the street kids.

During the cold, harsh winters when the temperatures dropped and the winds howled in the night, my dad brought home different families to sleep in our apartment. On those nights, my older brother and sister and I got to sleep on the living room carpet with the other kids. Their mothers or fathers got to sleep in our beds because "every adult has a right to dignity—poor or not poor." My father became really emphatic when he talked about dignity. "There is a limit to what you can take away from a man. If you take away his dignity, you might as well take away his soul."

My mom and maternal grandmother would bring food and clothes to the places where the street kids lived. Mom would boil chicken parts and fry dozens and dozens of potato latkes while grandma baked *rugelah* and blessed the food. Once we had to go behind the butcher store, down a wrought iron ladder in the ground, and into a boiler room. Two families were living down there without any beds or lights. I don't remember if they were Negroes or Jews. When we left my mother said, "They are human beings forced to live like alley cats." Then she cried for a long time. When we arrived home, she took her good Sabbath dress out of the closet and said, "Mrs. Lowe can wear this on open school night. Everyone should have a sense of dignity." My mother hugged and kissed me and called me her *shayna maydl*.

It was during these memorable days of my childhood that I came to understand the many manifestations of poverty—the hopelessness, the risk taking, the neglect, the need to stop feeling anything at all as a way of emotional survival. Homelessness, hunger, and pain were just the symptoms of a much bigger problem—a loss of dignity and the inability to ever, ever take "a step upward."

The number of "street kids" and homeless families has increased dramatically in recent years. The faces I see with empty eyes and straggled hair are not all that different from those faces that color my childhood memories.

Although my father passed away a decade ago, my mother continues to knit and hand-make clothes using the wool and fabric from remnants of the past. "Everything does not need to be machine made and brand new," she says. "Better it should be made with care and worn with dignity."

It is difficult to articulate my feelings about the plight of the downtrodden and the impoverished. Their chronic struggle to escape poverty with all its hidden trappings affects the way I live and certainly the way I teach. School-organized clothing and food drives and efforts to connect with other people who feel the way I do about assuming responsibility for impoverished children and their families are a part of my everyday world.

When I learned of Benjamin Franklin Day, a school that chose to break precedents in order to achieve a vision of how life might be, the stretch of space and time between the cities of New York and Seattle seemed no greater than the distance my father and I walked from Surf Avenue to Mermaid and down to Neptune Bay. I felt compelled to visit this school and better understand why and how one African-American woman principal battled the barriers of bureaucratization and tunnel vision in order to foster in both school and local community a collective responsibility for homeless children and their families.

As was the case each time I walked alongside my dad, hand in hand, I returned from my journey to Seattle feeling inspired and renewed. Once again, I saw that a caring heart, an outreached hand, and an unwavering respect for another man's dignity can change the world.

Above all, my belief in "the teacher" as a person of strength and hope was reaffirmed. My father was right. The world is bigger than Coney Island. It sure feels grand to take "a step upward," especially when I'm holding the hand of someone who can't take the step alone.

ACKNOWLEDGMENTS

This book represents so much of what life is about—struggle, introspection, and the tenacity of the human spirit. In many respects, it is a portrayal of who we are and who we can be.

The indefatigable qualities of those who dared to effect change, who reached beyond the real for the ideal, inspired the writing of this book. I wish to express my deep respect and appreciation to principal Carole Williams, Janet Jones Preston, Joe Garcia, Robert Mann, Diann Mize, Bev Parker, Simeon Fields, and so many others.

Countless people gave unstintingly of their time and insights in the telling of this miraculous story. Many are quoted and named in the book; many, to whom I pledged complete confidentiality, are quoted but not named. Numerous others who served as a rich source of information are not represented in fair proportion to their generosity. I am equally grateful to all.

This book was originally prepared as a Teachers College doctoral dissertation. Many thanks to Professor Linda Darling-Hammond and Professor Robert Crain for working alongside me throughout the progression of that successful academic accomplishment. Their belief in the importance of turning that dissertation into a Teachers College publication launched the writing of this book.

I can only begin to express my gratitude to Carole Saltz, who, as publisher of Teachers College Press, commissioned this work. Her commitment to the book revealed a passion for the subject of homeless children that closely parallels my own. Carole's faith in my ability to carry this project to completion sustained my determination to keep on writing.

Carol Collins, a brilliant editor at Teachers College Press, did the first editing that so greatly enhanced the quality of this text. It was done with a sensitive touch and a stroke of genius when placing pencil to paper.

Accomplished freelance editor Trudy Raschkind Steinfeld facilitated the necessary rewrites and refinements for the integration of additional information in the final version of this book.

Sue Roccuzzo, a dear friend and a kindred soul, accompanied me on my first trip to Seattle. She spent countless hours transcribing taped interviews and worked with me into the wee hours of the morning; her presence turned work into pleasure. There are no words to describe my gratitude for the many ways in which she stood by me.

Dr. Elana Elster, a challenging listener and a remarkably honest critic, supported me as one colleague does another through the difficult task of writing both dissertation and book. Her own work in the field of education is to be applauded.

Much love to my family, my friends, and my rabbi, Jacob Rubenstein, who all have been unfailing sources of joy, laughter, and strength.

CHAPTER 1

Introduction

In 1985, Carole Williams, an African-American woman in her mid-forties, assumed her first principalship at Benjamin Franklin Day Elementary School in Seattle. She had worked for 21 years in the Seattle school system as a paraprofessional, teacher, curriculum coordinator, and assistant and acting principal. But nothing she had experienced during that time had prepared her for B.F. Day.

The three-story brick building, constructed in 1892, was filled with eerie shadows cast from low-wattage bare bulbs landing on creaking wooden floors that had lost their varnished finish long ago. Doodles and initials of students from years past were gouged into the abraded lacquer of floor-bolted desks. Rusting radiators took a solid two days to generate heat as they drew upon a practically defunct boiler. The walls, a variety of glossy enameled paint colors, revealed the remnants of yellowed Scotch tape and metal staples.

Not only was the massive old building deteriorating physically; the school inside it was slowly dying, both academically and psychologically.

It consisted of two separate and distinctly unequal programs. An alternative program for kindergarten through fifth grade named Orca had been established by well-educated and involved neighborhood parents seeking to provide a "cut-above-the-rest" educational experience for their children. The self-contained program for 180 gifted students occupied classrooms on the main entry level. Supervised by an exceptionally strong parent/teacher body, Orca's literature, art, and music curriculums, national test scores, and expense budget reflected the epitome of a superbly designed academic program.

In sharp contrast, confined to a distinctly different atmosphere in the basement and on the second floor, 140 emotionally and socially needy children of color at risk of failure were secluded from their cream-of-the-crop counterparts. Constant altercations and violent outbursts

1

A shared learning experience: B. F. Day students, staff member Simeon Fields, and cooperating high school student "mentors" on a field trip to the University of Washington, led by Botany Greenhouse manager Doug Ewing. (Photo: Mike Siegel/*Seattle Times)*

were accepted as part of school life amidst this disturbed, anxious, and angry student body and their depressed and distraught teaching staff. To compound the situation, the Day student body lacked its first and second graders, who were bused to another school to accommodate laws on "racial balancing."

In assuming the principalship at B.F. Day, Carole Williams took on the challenge of overseeing what she perceived as a combat zone between "the haves" and "the have nots." Disparate in every respect, the two programs nevertheless shared one building and one principal. Stereotypes were reinforced on the schoolyard as the Orca children attempted to steer clear of their less-than-desirable schoolmates. Pushing, shoving, teasing, and name calling were an inherent part of recess.

For the first year or two, Carole did not feel secure enough to break down the physical and psychological walls that served to separate Orca from Day children. Then, in the late spring of 1988, an incident occurred that would lead Carole to question her role as the principal of a school divided. Following an altercation during recess between Orca and Day children at the main water fountain on the first floor, Orca's head teacher approached Carole and suggested that the Day children use only the water fountain on the second floor. In the hope of curtailing the pushing, shoving, and disparaging remarks, Carole agreed to inform all Day children that they were no longer permitted to use "Orca's water fountain." After recess, Day children were instructed to use the water fountain on the second floor only.

Carole returned to the privacy of her office and cried. She knew she had betrayed the children of Day:

> I forgot who I was there for. For whose betterment did I say that Day kids couldn't get a drink from Orca's water fountain? The children occupying the second floor and the basement already believed themselves to be second-class citizens and of the wrong color. As a black woman in a position of authority, I had just confirmed their own lack of worth.

The following day, Carole assembled all the Day children and publicly apologized. She admitted to having made a very poor and ungrounded decision. Day children needed an identity, and Carole was now determined to change this inequity between "the nation's best" and "the school's worst."

In the days and weeks that followed, Carole began to make many house calls preceding and following school hours and discovered an unidentified group of homeless and deeply impoverished children. Families appeared to be living in cars, garages, and even under bridges. Although Carole was well aware that such situations existed, seeing it up close, rather than through the lens of a television camera, led her to question her role as principal as well as that of her school.

A majority of Day students were overwhelmed with a multitude of personal and family problems over which they had little control. On those days they attended class, they were often hungry, exhausted, or inappropriately dressed for the weather. Many children were worried about where they would spend the night and with whom. All these issues seemed to take the form of depression or disruptive and defiant behavior.

Once Carole began to look at the harsh social realities that loomed just beyond school doors, she began to understand the antisocial interactions rampant between students and between students and teachers.

The school building was slated for a $5-million renovation in the fall of 1989, but it was difficult to envision any "rebirth" for a large number of its students. Of the 350 children enrolled, 175 were from single-parent families; 140 were classified as low income; 100 were living in housing projects, transitional housing (motels), or emergency shelters; 50 children were at high risk of failure; and 25 were being monitored for abuse and neglect by Seattle's Department of Social and Health Services. Sixteen foreign languages were spoken by the children, and 60% of their families were at or below the poverty level. Over a period of 18 months, three children tried to kill themselves at school, and several others threatened to do so.

As Carole recalled one child's suicide attempt and the way it influenced her view of the school, she captured the moment of awakening in which she acknowledged that the seemingly separate realities of school and home life are in fact inextricably intertwined:

> It seemed to be a typical day in which I was ready to throw up my hands before putting out the next brushfire. But suddenly I heard this terrible commotion in the main hallway. A little boy was standing on top of the third floor landing ready to jump. I can still see his sad eyes and his trembling body. He was tiny but really a handsome little boy who very rarely smiled and was very quiet. At times, for no apparent reason, he would explode. He seemed like such a loveless child, as did so many of the other children.
>
> Looking up from the main floor landing, I experienced a surge of panic. I thought, "Dear Lord, please help this poor baby. He's only a little boy." Then, almost out of nowhere a teacher appeared behind the child and grabbed him off the railing. Here

was this young boy who should be so full of life but instead experienced such pain, such hopelessness that he could find no other way out than suicide.

At that moment, I was jolted into the social reality of a small child's life. Had he been neglected or abused? Was his family life in a state of chaos and turmoil? Did he live with his mother, his grandmother, a foster parent? Did he have a home? I couldn't answer any of these questions.... In that chilling moment of desperation, I knew I needed help....

That night, I tossed and turned as that small child's suicide attempt became an incessant instant replay triggering the same surge of fear and panic....

Who was responsible for the well-being of this child?... If this child could recite his times tables, if he could rattle off the definition of a thousand vocabulary words, or spell every multisyllabic word in *Webster's Dictionary,* could the school proudly proclaim to have met its responsibility as an educational institution? Did it matter if this child was hungry or tired or homeless? Did it matter if he was unloved and uncared for? Was the school going to meet this child's unmet needs or was that outside the domain of an excellent education?

I thought about the unkempt and unruly boys in the schoolyard. Perhaps all of them were crying for help in the only way they knew how. Why should they respect the very people who could help them survive emotionally but chose rather to comfortably and narrowly focus on purely academic matters?

This was the culmination of too many past moments in which I critically questioned my role, my sense of direction, my purpose as a principal. This was the moment that I questioned the role of this school, of any school. No longer could I think of Benjamin Franklin Day as an island unaffected by the mainland just a few miles away. I could no longer think of the school as solely an educational agency. Nor could I continue to play the role of a bureaucratic administrator....

If this school was going to change its course and assume more than academic responsibility for its students, it would require a collaboration of minds, hearts, and hands. Of this, I was sure....

From that moment on, Carole Williams became dedicated to creating that collaboration. With new colleagues from other public and private agencies, parents, and community activists of all ethnic and professional backgrounds, she and her staff transformed first themselves and then their school into a model of educational success. Ranked lowest in academic improvement in the 1988–89 school year among the 65 elementary schools in Seattle, by the 1990–91 school year B.F. Day ranked 7th in improvement in reading, 16th in language arts, and 18th in math, which the school district acknowledged as "a compelling record of success."

Their tools were: a new vision of themselves and what they could accomplish; a totally new program they named KOOL-IS—Kids Organized On Learning In School—that focuses not only on schooling but also on housing and jobs; a forum called the Site Council, which deals with issues of the entire school and community from long-range planning to interpersonal relationships; sponsorship and training by major corporations; collaboration with the local university and high schools; and vigorous outreach and fund raising.

This book is the story of why and how this urban public school assumed ownership of the problems of its homeless students and their families and assumed responsibility for correcting social ills and building a better society. It is, therefore, the story of two theories in action: purposing and social reconstructionism. Professionals and community members converted the school from an exclusively educational institution into both an educational and social service agency with coherent short- and long-term goals.

Before focusing on B.F. Day's remarkable story, it is necessary to take a step back and look at why the school was in such dire straits to begin with. For that, one must address the issues of poverty, homelessness, and racism.

CHAPTER 2

Schooling Children of Poverty

Across this nation, thousands upon thousands of homeless children are growing up unnurtured, unloved, and uneducated. Until recently, federal, state, and local agencies have demonstrated more constraint than facilitation in addressing the profound educational and social challenges homeless children present for urban, suburban, and rural neighborhood schools.

As it was excluded minority, handicapped, and at-risk children who desperately sought legal rights to free, appropriate public education in the 1970s and 1980s, so it is homeless children who seek ground-breaking precedents upon schoolhouse steps in the 1990s. Unfortunately, lessons of the past resound in the present: Overcoming barriers to school enrollment and gaining access to an educative institution do not necessarily translate into a fruitful learning experience. For even after facilitating decisions are issued by the judiciary, and even after enabling legislation is passed by Congress and state legislatures, the reality of effecting "meaningful change" rests with school districts, principals, teachers, parents, and students. In the final analysis, social problems that were originally acknowledged as issues under the schoolhouse roof must be resolved at this same site.

THE ISSUE OF SOCIAL DISLOCATION

The cumulative effects of historical racial subjugation in American society are played out daily by a large underclass in central cities (Wilson, 1987). Educational, social, and economic dislocation have become automatically associated with people of color, who have been compelled to maintain marginal positions in a class-stratified society. Low aspirations, high dropout rates, substance abuse, teenage pregnancy, female-headed households, joblessness, welfare dependency, and homelessness seem

7

Simeon Fields, KOOL-IS case manager, with B. F. Day students: "All children come to school with a natural curiosity and eagerness to learn. Nourishing that curiosity is vital."

to be the fate of children born in ghetto communities. Inferior economic status, negative neighborhood identification, and chronic social-class subordination contribute to a poor sense of self, family instability, and behavioral pathology (Natriello, McDill, & Pallas, 1990).

Although twentieth-century educators can proudly state that children of all races, classes, religions, and ethnic backgrounds have been eligible for enrollment and have in fact attended common elementary schools, there has always existed a structural segmentation of students according to race and ethnicity that has seemed to contribute to—and possibly foster—a sense of social dislocation (Tyack, 1974). The "commonness" of the public school has been severely limited, as Cremin (1988) observes:

> by the de jure segregation of black children in the South and of Native American children in the West, by the de facto segregation of black and Puerto Rican children in the North, of Chicano children in the Southwest, and of Asian children in the Far West, and by the segregation and tracking of inner-city children according to criteria that frequently stressed social class background. (p. 551)

For most children of color, common schools fostered the very inequalities they were designed to prevent—social stratification as well as regional and racial segregation. According to Diane Ravitch (1985):

> Where educational oppression of a minority was blatant and purposeful, as in the case of the American Indian, the policy was a disaster that neither educated nor assimilated.... While some were "weaned away from the blanket," as the saying went, most simply developed a strong internal resistance to the new behavior....
>
> The case of black educational history [differs].... Whereas government policy attempted to force the assimilation and de-ethnicization of the Indians, it explicitly sought to prevent the assimilation of blacks. Whereas the cultural aspirations of European immigrant groups were at least tolerated and frequently encouraged, those of blacks were ignored, or worse, mocked. (pp. 192, 197)

In 1954, the president of the New York City Board of Education verbalized what most educators across the country already knew—that "a psychological scarring" happened to children of color. Segregation, whether overt or covert, "damaged the personality of minority group children," "decreased their motivation," and "impaired their ability to learn" (Ravitch, 1985, p. 237).

Four decades later, public schools continue to grapple with issues of race, ethnicity, religion, and social class. Today, however, a new breed of person called "the homeless student," known in familiar circles as "the shelter rat," leads to yet another form of minority discrimination and seg- regation. While there are those who believe that homeless students must be mainstreamed, there are others who argue that separate schools, often sited at the shelter itself, are best suited to meet the wide array of needs unique to the homeless child. The question remains whether Native Americans, African-Americans, and Asian-Americans, among other minorities across the country, will continue to be short-changed through yet a new form of discrimination: not by race but by housing status.

Despite the time it has taken for educators to recognize this prob- lem, it is clear to students in these minority groups from the moment they enter school. The issue was stated succinctly for me by a young man, of Native American descent, perhaps in his late teens, whom I found sitting on a street curb just outside the Farmer's Market, a tourist attraction in downtown Seattle. He was wearing jeans that were torn at the knee and rather frayed around the ankles, where they met a pair of leather boots. A stone-washed denim jacket partially covered a white tank top, and an engraved belt provided the finishing touch to a gen- erally slipshod look. His shoulder-length hair hung loosely around rather pronounced cheekbones, a chiseled nose, and deep-set eyes, and he strummed the nylon strings of an old guitar with long, thin fingers. His name was Kyle. Well aware that he was "one hell of a sight—the city thinks I detract from the tourist trade," Kyle told me about him- self, his ancestral lineage, an array of reasons for dropping out of high school. He asked me some questions about my study and challenged my sincerity and concern regarding homeless people. Finally, he asked me to "jot this down for posterity":

> Native Americans, African-Americans, Asian-Americans lost their homes and their sense of place over the course of the last two centuries. Homelessness is not new to them. It is only new to those people who are waking up from a collective amnesia.
>
> As long as the schools continue to teach social inequality by the very way they treat kids every single moment of the day, act- ing as if kids' personal and social problems are invisible, this country will continue to sleepwalk.
>
> You say you want to bring about some kind of change in the schools. Start by putting a sign over the entrance of every school building that reads: "School May Be Harmful to Your Emotional and Social Well-Being. Enter at Your Own Risk. This School Does Not Assume Responsibility for Your Sense of Belonging or Your Sense of Place."

CONTEMPORARY HOMELESSNESS

There are direct parallels between our current economic adversity and homelessness and those of the Great Depression. As it was then, so it is now that the soup kitchen lines appear in towns and cities across this nation. Like the uprooted migrants of the Dust Bowl in the 1930s, many families today are loading dilapidated cars and vans with their meager belongings and going off in search of a place called "home." Dispossessed, thousands of families seek a place to live, a place to work, a place to build a life.

The number of homeless families appears to have begun to increase during the early recession years of 1981 and 1982. Following farm foreclosures and urban gentrification, many young mothers lost their partners and sense of identity, and children were separated from their neighborhoods, close friends, and schools. However, unlike the endemic homelessness of the Okies as portrayed by John Steinbeck in *The Grapes of Wrath,* homelessness in the 1980s and 1990s is not confined to any particular geographic location; it is, rather, spread across the nation.

Dusted out and tractored out, the Okies were drawn west in search of work and land on which to build a home. The typology of today's homeless presents a more kaleidoscopic sequence of events that lead to homelessness, as families intentionally leave a permanent residence to escape domestic violence, crime, and drug-ridden neighborhoods, to seek better employment opportunities. Their new destination is strongly influenced by the promise of a job, the proximity of relatives who might provide temporary housing, or the vision of a better life. But as resources diminish and "doubling up" proves problematic, families become homeless in what they had hoped would be "the promised land" (Hagen & Ivanoff, 1988; van Ry, 1990).

The escalating visibility of single mothers with preschool and school-age children living on the streets, in welfare hotels, and in emergency shelters is perhaps the most distinguishing attribute of contemporary homelessness. If current trends continue, school-age children will constitute the largest and fastest-growing segment of the homeless population by the year 2000 (National Center for Children in Poverty, 1990). Nationwide estimates of the number of homeless school-age children vary radically, according to recent publications of factual and statistical reports by the Children's Defense Fund (1991). Based on city and state surveys, as well as estimates from across the country, a U.S. Department of Education (1989) report asserts that there are 273,000 homeless school-age children, the majority of whom are clustered in inner cities and about one-third of whom do not attend school on a regular basis. But the

National Coalition for the Homeless (1990) estimates that there are at least 500,000 to 750,000 homeless children and that less than half of them attend school regularly due to a lack of clothing, food, and sleep. In this way, childhood destitution and illiteracy seem to preserve and perpetuate each other across generations, regardless of race, language, or culture.

Responding to the legal rights of impoverished children, the Stewart B. McKinney Homeless Assistance Act of 1987 (P. L. 100-77), a federal law, included a section that addresses the educational needs of homeless children. Mandating revision of state- and local-level school residency laws, the McKinney Act proclaimed that schools could no longer deny access to homeless students who did not have proof of residency within the school's zone. Homeless parents and students might choose to remain at the school the child attended before becoming homeless or to transfer to the school nearest the temporary shelter. In the former situation, the student's school district was required to provide transportation from the shelter or hotel to the school. Moreover, the state was to assure that local schools would accommodate students "in keeping with the best interest of the child," rather than on the basis of administrative convenience or cost.

Despite overwhelming need, change was slow in coming. According to the Children's Defense Fund (1991), three-fifths of the states had not even begun to demonstrate any compliance with this law by the end of 1989. By 1990, a raised consciousness led to the McKinney Amendments, which broadened the original Act of 1987 to ensure that all states take a closer, harder look at any school policies or practices that might "act as a barrier to the enrollment, attendance, or success in school of homeless children and homeless youth" (McKinney Act, Sec. 612, amending Sec. 721).

Educational and social reform mandated on a national level does not ensure lasting and continuous improvements in the human condition. Although uniformity, expedience, and compliance with mandated change can be institutionalized, the individual and subjective meaning and development of change escapes tangible enforcement, whether by reward or by punishment (Passow, 1984). As Fullan (1991) states, "[Educational] reform is badly needed, yet people's experience with change is overwhelmingly negative—imposition is the norm, costs outweigh benefits, the few successes are short lived" (p.353).

SOCIAL AND PSYCHOLOGICAL ISSUES

The ill effects suffered by homeless children are given extraordinary expression in the following verbatim transcription. My tape recorder, already running to record another conversation, captured the volatile emotions of an 11-year-old girl who was approached by a social worker at an emergency shelter:

> You think you know what homeless mean but you don't know nothin' 'bout homeless. You think homeless mean you ain't got no apartment, you ain't got no bed for yourself, ain't got no place to wash off when you soil or you be sweaty. Well, bein' homeless mean more than all that.
>
> It mean you don't got no next-door neighbor, no best friend no more. You don't got no favorite place to play or hide your candy money. You don't even got your own seat in your own classroom, you be movin' so many time. Don't know the teacher name. So who care? She don't know your name either.
>
> You ain't got no good memories of holidays or the movies or even rides. You ain't even got yourself bad memories. You know why? You bet you don't! 'Cause one shelter look like the next, and soon you can't remember how long you been in this one or that one. Anyway, it don't make no difference. Not after a whiles it don't. You know why? 'Cause you be doublin' up so many nights in the same bed covers, sharin' the same potty so many nights, that one mornin' you wake up and you ain't sure who you is anymore. Maybe you still you, maybe you turn into the other person.
>
> So don't tell me you knows 'bout homeless kids. And don't ask me if I understand what happenin' to my family bein' we got no home. They invisible and so is me. I not here anymore. I died three year ago. Hey, you wastin' your time talkin' to a dead person.

Children of poverty often mirror the depression, rage, and mental anguish of their primary caretaker. They also are disproportionately destined to experience a myriad of antisocial problems that lead to a sense of failure in their early school years (Bassuk & Gallagher, 1990; J. Hall & Maza, 1990; Natriello et al. 1990). Since homeless students are often compelled to change shelters and schools several times during any one year, they never stay in one place long enough to attain a sense of belonging. Those small possessions that connect them to their past are left behind.

Students and their entire families often share one small room when residing in hotels or motels, or experience noisy barracks-like conditions in overcrowded shelters. Frequently, access to and use of community medical and mental health services are undermined by lengthy paperwork, inadequate payment coverage, or plain fear. Potential recipients often forgo such necessary treatment as prescription drugs, immunizations, and therapy. This lack of physical and mental health care often accounts for poor school attendance. When children do attend class, they are often stressed out, hungry, exhausted, and dressed inappropriately for the weather. Emotional and socialization problems may show up as depression or aggression in class. These transient and frightened students are often embarrassed to tell anyone at school about their lifestyle and the stress and turmoil they experience (U.S. Department of Education, 1989).

Social injustice is often perpetuated by blaming the victim. "By making believe that failure is something that kids do, as different from how it is something done to them, and then by explaining their failure in terms of other things they do, we likely contribute to the maintenance of school failure" (McDermott, 1987, p. 363).

RESPONSIVE SCHOOLING FOR CHILDREN OF POVERTY

Throughout our nation's history, public schools have been compelled to become agents of social change: institutions concerned with poverty, social welfare, and reform. So it is no surprise that the controversial debate about socially and emotionally responsive schooling for children of poverty was one of the four top issues in the 1992 presidential campaign, appearing as a major theme in numerous gubernatorial and legislative races as well. Across the country, many stressed the urgent need for radical reforms, including "break-the-mold" experimental schools that would diverge from 50 years of "conventional wisdom" regarding effective delivery of both educational and social services in roughly 16,000 school districts (Wirt & Kirst, 1992, pp. 2–3).

However, despite the buzzwords and grand schemes, change is slow to come. Social and economic realities of communities differ, and so do the educational and local leaders. Therefore, step-by-step implementation of a plan for accommodating the needs of homeless students is difficult, and perhaps impractical, to prescribe on a national scale.

Bureaucratic entanglement impedes services to the homeless and truly disadvantaged. Mental health and medical intervention programs provide too little too late, and efforts of social service agencies are often piecemeal, uncoordinated, and duplicative. Agencies and schools are often not allowed to share information about one another's respective "clients," even when those clients are a parent and child who are part of the same family unit (Molnar, 1988).

The bureaucratic intransigence of these divided social agencies virtually guarantees a lack of comprehensive services (Tobis, 1985). At present, no central office is responsible for coordinating a comprehensive, ongoing array of services to vulnerable families at critical moments in their lives.

Recently, the role of establishing a focal point for leadership on this issue has been assumed by a number of boards of education and public schools across the nation (*Homewords,* 1991). The National Association of State Coordinators for the Education of Homeless Children and Youth, formed in 1989, assumed responsibility for evaluating and implementing special services that fall under the education component of the federal McKinney Act. The following excerpt from their publication, titled *In the Shadow of Opportunity: Removing Barriers and Creating Success for America's Homeless Children and Youth* (1992), leads one's thoughts back to Kyle, the homeless high school dropout who so adeptly criticized schools for not providing a "sense of belonging":

> Perhaps the greatest challenge facing educators in the 1990s is providing a stable and continuous education to homeless children and youth. There are an estimated 317,197 school-age children and youth in homeless families each year. These children live with the daily uncertainties of where they will sleep, when and what they will eat, and whether they will have adequate clothing—the basic necessities of life....
>
> Homeless children have the same needs as other children. They need understanding, love, and acceptance. They need a place to call home and a sense of belonging to a neighborhood and school. While no substitute for a permanent home, school can offer the continuity, security, and normalcy in a child's otherwise turbulent life. (p. 1)

With individual and collective resolve, scattered public schools in different states are attempting to provide a sense of acceptance, nurturance, and belonging for their homeless students. This clearly involves enlightening and educating teachers about the plight of such children and their families. It also involves creating opportunities for a running dialogue about how schools might restructure their schedules, social organization, and functions in order to best meet the needs of children who have no sense of self or place.

The number of schools employing noteworthy strategies in this quest is unknown. Information from state and regional coordinators of homeless programs (Center for Law and Education, 1990) suggests that school responsiveness varies from excellent to poor to nonexistent. Information exchange and networking between individual schools across states and even within states is limited.

Orchestrating collaboration within a community depends greatly on the social composition of the school and the leadership abilities of the principal and staff. The overriding mission, a challenge for many concerned educators, is to empower school and community to assume a collective responsibility in meeting the basic needs of the at-risk students who comprise the transient homeless population. To be sure, what works in one school may not work or be needed or be appropriate in another. But when change is tied closely to real unmet needs, both schools and parents are motivated to design their own innovative problem-solving policy (Marsh & Bowman, 1988). Even less-well-educated communities can become effective participants in programs for needy students if the "bias of neglect" is overcome and information is disseminated throughout the neighborhood (Berman, McLaughlin, Pincus, Weiler, & Williams, 1979).

If, on the other hand, a school is motivated not by a real need for change but by an opportunity to reap the benefits of bureaucratic funding by setting up a program for homeless, bilingual, or handicapped students, it is unlikely that the program will succeed.(Firestone, 1989; Crandell, Eiseman & Louis, 1986).

WHAT ARE SCHOOLS FOR?

The first page of John Goodlad's book, *What Schools Are For* (1979), reads:

> Addressing the White House Conference on Education ... Vice President Hubert Humphrey proclaimed that we would go down in history as the nation that used its educational system to deal successfully with the problems of poverty, unemployment, slum clearance, and, indeed, world peace. Is this what schools are for?

Goodlad suggests three major subquestions to the main question: What are schools expected or asked to do? What do schools do? What should schools do? He responds:

> Agreement on the school as the place "where it all comes together" and the place to engage in a collaborative process of improvement does not require agreement on a common theory of schooling. But it does force greater attention to the school's present condition, and the quality of life there....
>
> Those who are more concerned about the health, happiness, and safety of their children will find plenty of opportunities to work toward a more wholesome school environment. (p. 83)

Presented with the question "What are schools for?" each of us must first consider our basic assumptions and expectations. If we perceive the school as an integral part of the surrounding community, reflecting the social and economic issues of the neighborhood culture, then the school assumes a central role. It becomes an organ of the community, with a continuous flow of ideas and people into and through it—an open system. However, if we think only in terms of students, teachers, principals, administrators, and boards of education, we unwittingly create an enclosed system from which parents, doctors, social workers, businesses, and innumerable, interactive agencies are barred.

Seymour Sarason (1982) has argued that through acculturation, most of us do, in fact, conceptualize the educational scene as encapsulated and sharply delineated within the walls of a school building. We see schools as "oases of learning shielded from [their] social surround" (p. 18). We distance ourselves from the social realities just beyond the school doors and maintain the traditional view of the school as part of a closed system that is functionally and administratively distinct from the societal dynamics of groups and agencies outside that system.

When Sarason asks, "Does it make sense to talk about schools as if they are part of a closed system...?" the implied answer is "no." To place distance between the school setting and the community culture within which a school physically resides is to obscure the communication that is so vital to establishing and achieving educational objectives that support family and community life. It is only through an ongoing dialogue between the school and its surrounding community culture that the school can construct its open, twofold role as both recipient and provider of education.

The school must first learn from those it wishes to teach, so that the community's valued collective perspective regarding the purpose of schooling is clear. The school should not, therefore, be viewed as the quintessential designer and provider of a cognitive map to be learned, memorized, and permanently adhered to by the people of a culture. "For people are not just map readers; they are map makers as well. People are cast out into imperfectly charted, continually shifting seas of everyday life. Mapping them out is a constant process." (Frake, 1977, p. 6).

The school must explore the terrain beyond its walls and doors if it is to work from a set of principles for map making that are compatible with the cultural milieu in which its students are navigators. To view neighborhood life through the eyes of the community is quite different than to view it through school-colored window panes (Wilson, 1987).

CHAPTER 3

The Principal with a Vision

Carole William's courageous exploration of the community's terrain, and her unflinching appraisal of what she found there, led her not only to a new view of neighborhood life but also to a new vision of her own role and potential and those of her staff.

Numerous studies show that the initiation and successful implementation of change in school are most likely to occur with the presence of a strong, trusted, and supportive advocate, generally the principal (Huberman & Miles, 1986; Louis & Miles, 1990; Smith & Andrews, 1989). Although principals' styles of leadership might vary greatly from school to school (Andrews, 1988; Andrews, Soder, & Jacoby, 1986), the effective principal has a vision and is able to articulate and communicate that vision clearly. "The principal's day to day behavior communicates that she has a firm understanding of the purpose of schooling and can translate that meaning into programs and activities within the school" (Smith & Andrews, 1989, p. 15).

Effective leaders have a way of helping individuals rise above the routine of daily classroom life. They are able to envision a more exciting and enticing way of doing things. "They urge people to go beyond the routine—to break out of the mold into something more lively and vibrant" (Smith & Andrews, 1989, p. 17).

A TIME OF AWAKENING

In her attempt to become a more effective principal, Carole tried to determine why life at B.F. Day was so dysfunctional. She started close to home; one did not need to look farther than the schoolyard to see just how bad things were.

Joe Garcia, director of the Atlantic Street Center, a social service

B. F. Day principal Carole Williams: "If another school wishes to repli-
cate what we are doing, . . . [they] will have to restructure their
thought processes regarding the school as an institution of education."
(Photo: Jim Bates/*Education Week)*

agency in Seattle, and codeveloper in 1989 of B.F. Day's KOOL-IS (Kids Organized On Learning In School) program, recalled the situation this way:

> There were about 10 to 12 young, black males who appeared to control the building. The school yard was not all that different from the yard of a penitentiary. In most prisons, the yard is controlled by a handful of men, and nothing occurs without the okay of these leaders. The B.F. Day playground was a sure facsimile of the finest penitentiary yard on the West Coast. Here were the makings of a future reformatory population acting out a slang form of leadership.
>
> This small, but devious, group of males controlled the building, the hallways, the lunchroom, bathrooms, even classrooms through a circuitous form of intimidation. There were assigned spotters and runners positioned in doorways, stairwells, and outside classroom and office doors.
>
> Teachers who had exerted disciplinary action in days past were identified and targeted. Rocks were thrown into the windshields and windows of staff cars. Tires were punctured or slashed.... Sometimes, verbal threats were shouted by some faceless figure in a distant shadow. In this way, direct intimidation let teachers know exactly who was in charge in this school, regardless of bureaucratic opinion.
>
> Most of these boys were later identified as homeless or as occupants of transitional shelters. Most of them had been neglected, abused, or abandoned by either one or both parents. The fact remained that what went on in the lives of these children before and after school hours directly impacted upon those hours between 9:00 and 3:00, whether the principal and teachers recognized it or not.

Within the building, exclusionary practices seemed to be the customary survival route for teachers, who placed even moderately disruptive children outside the classroom door, banned them from gym, art, music, drama, and special assemblies, or condemned them to a corner of the classroom so they might be denounced and ridiculed. For these children—perceived as "trouble makers," "impossible," "delinquent," or "undesirable"—the school day often translated into rejection and humiliation. Such children assumed a sprawling posture on hallway floors or stairwells just beyond the classroom door, or loped the corridors for lengthy periods of time. Tension and distress abounded; the "school losers" continued to make their presence known, even when not in the classroom, by sticking gum on water fountain faucets, stuffing urinals with tissue paper, or otherwise defacing school or staff property.

The teachers' exclusionary practices merely elicited further adverse reactions on the part of the students they disciplined, as well as fostering a contagious distrust and alienation among the school staff and the student body. Each group clearly perceived the other as "the enemy"; each anticipated, expected, and was prepared for altercations.

The same group of disruptive children would be sent to the principal's office several times each day. B.F. Day's family support worker, Janet Jones Preston, who joined the school in September 1988, later described this phenomenon as one in which "teachers seemed to want the children 'fixed' or 'altered,' then sent back to class ready to concentrate and learn."

Carole began to feel overwhelmed by "an escalating rate of violence and vandalism as well as a rampant absenteeism on the part of both mischievous students and irascible teachers." Consumed by a growing, pervasive sense that she could not shoulder all the responsibility for necessary change, Carole struggled to maintain "an appearance of administrative propriety." She often spoke with teachers about such inappropriate disciplinary action as "kicking a child out of the room or conveying by way of disparaging remarks that the child was a lost cause." She spent the rest of her time "putting out one brushfire after another" as she attempted to quell the anger of distrusting students and regain order "by assuming the role of surrogate mother, psychologist, mediator, and sometimes judge and jury." Nevertheless, the sometimes deleterious behavior of both students and teachers "seemed to undermine any movement toward a harmonious school climate."

Carole and her staff were aware that a great many of the students' lives were fraught with family chaos of one type or another. However, they had never explicitly recognized that it was often the home life experiences of these students that underlay their defiant and disruptive behavior.

One afternoon, one of the school bus drivers refused to start the bus unless a belligerent boy and his sister were immediately removed. Carole recollected the situation with unrestrained emotion and tears during an informal interview:

> I decided to remove the children from the bus and drive them home myself. I remember looking at both children and wondering how such fragile little people could cause such chaos on a school bus....

As we drove up to their apartment building, there were three or four police cars in front with the sirens going and the lights flashing. The little boy placed his hands over his head and started to cry aloud, "Oh, no, no, no! Not this again. This happens all the time. I'm so afraid. I just want to hide under my bed until the sirens go away." This was one of many drug busts in which this child's mother was involved....

This rude awakening led me to think about the children and their behavior problems in a very different way.... The pugnacious student behavior was, in fact, a manifestation of the harsh realities and life experiences that preceded and followed school hours.

On the day she assumed the principalship, Carole had assumed responsibility for the well-being of many young children. Although she was a credentialed administrator, she had little training in the moral, social, and psychological development of children at risk of failure. Concerning these children, her social and behavioral science background was long in theory but short in application.

Fully awakened to the overwhelming needs of many of the students, and frantic about the suicide attempts described in Chapter 1, Carole found that her vision of her own responsibility and commitment had become crystal clear. With a great sense of urgency, she set about awakening and refocusing the vision of her staff.

RELINQUISHING THE BURDEN OF PRESUMED COMPETENCE

Roland Barth, author of *Improving Schools from Within* (1990) captures the essence of the process Carole and her staff were about to embark on together: "The moment of greatest learning for any of us is when we find ourselves responsible for a problem that we care desperately to resolve. Then we need and seek out assistance. We are ready to learn" (p. 136).

Determined that the school must act as both a social and educational service agency, and acknowledging that the principal alone could not fully generate and control every aspect of such a school, Carole focused on both the emotional and moral inclusion of teachers, parents, and social service personnel. She believed that the best way to empower the multitude toward achieving a common purpose was to tap into and harness "the heart, soul, and good conscience of mature adults who impact ever so strongly upon the lives of young children."

Sergiovanni (1984) describes the effective principal as the "high priest" who leads others to have faith in the enduring values, beliefs, and cultural strands that are the essence of a school's individual identity. "The leader stands for certain ideals and principles which become cornerstones of their very being" (p. 109). Similarly, in describing the principal as the school's "moral authority," Lieberman and Miller (1984) stated: "Principals can maintain neutrality and let things progress as they always have; even that is a moral statement. Or they may take an active stance, threatening the assumptions of staff members and moving a school in more progressive or more regressive directions" (p. 76).

To be sure, the principal's actions, more than what he or she says, determine whether an ideology or vision involving change is to be taken seriously. If the principal verbally supports a change but does not actively engage in the implementation of that change, the chances for success appear limited. It is often for this reason that the implementation of an idea or goal succeeds in one school while failing in another located just a few blocks away (Berman & McLaughlin, 1977; Fullan, 1982; G. Hall & Griffin, 1980).

Carole's strong desire to help the students attending B.F. Day compelled her to ask the teachers and staff for help. One by one, she told me, "[I spoke to] the veterans and the sink-or-swim novices in the privacy of my home or office and expressed my desperation to help the homeless children and their families."

The inherent advantages of asking for assistance are succinctly stated by Barth (1990):

> Principals who always know how to do something perpetuate that "burden of presumed competence." A principal is hired from among 100 candidates because the selection committee supposes he or she knows how to do it. Therefore, for principals to admit that they do not know how is a sign of weakness, at best, and incompetence at worst....
>
> This declaration by the principal becomes a powerful invitation to teachers. It suggests that the principal and school need help, and that the teacher can provide the help. And it gives the teacher room to risk not knowing how either and perhaps to fail. More likely, the teacher can emerge a genuinely helpful leader of the school and friend and colleague of the principal. *I don't know how* is an attractive, disarming and realistic invitation likely to be accepted and handled with responsibility—and with collegiality. (pp. 139–140)

One of the special education teachers, Susan Stockfeld, a woman in her late twenties, corroborated Barth's notions as she described her reaction to Carole's initial requests for help:

> The general public may assume that teachers have the skills necessary to deal with economically impoverished children. The reality is that most teachers don't have those skills. They need to learn about poverty and how to cope with the side effects that

such conditions elicit in children such as distractibility, anxiety, depression, anger, and hostility....

The year that Carole asked the teachers to "help her help the children," I had 12 Special Ed children in my room, among whom 4 were homeless.... I thought, "If the principal can admit that she doesn't have all the answers, then so can I." On those days that were really difficult, which was just about every day, I knew I could go to Carole and find an authentic empathy and understanding for the way I felt. I might be frightened, frustrated, angry, or all of the above. At those times, Carole made it clear that she had often experienced similar emotions and it was okay....

I recall one particular occasion when I was down and out. I just didn't know what to do anymore. Carole took both my hands in hers and said, "I'm not concerned about what other teachers or administrators are going to say when they hear me shout, 'I don't know what to do! I need help!' So don't you be concerned either. Because you know what? The truth is that we all need help at one time or another whether we are courageous enough to admit it or not." From that day on, I didn't think twice about saying the "H" word—Help!

LEADERSHIP THAT BONDS PEOPLE TOGETHER IN A COMMON CAUSE

Having set in motion at least the beginnings of a social climate in which it was okay to admit that you were *not* okay, Carole's next move was to create a powerful moral bond among teachers, parents, and social service personnel that would draw them together toward a common cause. To do this, she actively evoked and sustained images and expectations of what an ideal school life might be like.

First and foremost, Carole established her own sincerity and seriousness of intent, as the following excerpts from numerous interviews with teachers, social service personnel, and school volunteers show:

TEACHER: Carole became the embodiment of a social morality that could not be challenged in good conscience.... She fueled a sense of what was ethically right and intrinsically wrong as she imbued each teacher with the values, beliefs, and convictions that sustained her own perseverance and psychological strength.... She painted an irresistible picture of what school life could and should be like.

FAMILY SUPPORT WORKER: Carole has never hesitated to talk about
the social injustice inflicted upon people of color. She always
says, "Wouldn't it be wonderful if we could just get past the
shallow generalizations and get to know people as very distinct and unique individuals in their own right?"... I see this
as the spiritual core of this gentle woman. And I suppose it is
from this core that she is able to energize those around her
to look at the world of children and the world of schooling
in a rather nontraditional way.

COMMUNITY VOLUNTEER: As a black, female principal, Carole
Williams conveys an aura in which it is virtually impossible
to relate to her as an administrative head. She presents herself as a caring and sincere woman first and a determined
professional second. You can't help but get to know her and
like her because she does not present herself as "the principal"; she is genuinely and simply Carole: a black woman
with a strong moral commitment to the well-being and education of homeless children and their families.

TEACHER: As a socially and morally reflective person, Carole has
somehow managed to bring out this same quality in every
teacher who has come to know her and to understand the
kind of morality she values and practices every day of her
life.... When I think of Carole Williams, I do not think of
"principal"; instead, I find myself thinking about "principle."

Amitai Etzioni (1988) explored this moral dimension in administrative roles and its motivational impact. While acknowledging an individual's psychological needs for esteem, autonomy, and self-actualization, Etzioni creates a compelling case for emotion, morality, and social
bonds as the sources of motivation.

It appears that what counts most to people is how they feel, what
they believe, and the moral values they share with their group leader and
group peers. When moral authority is asserted, a shared covenant or value
system begins to bond principal and teacher in moral commitment.

Even before the term KOOL-IS had been coined, its underlying ideology had been conveyed to the school staff on a one-to-one basis, as
well as collectively. Initial responses to Carole's ideas ranged from sar-
casm, doubt, and mistrust to reluctant agreement. Nonetheless, teachers did begin to share their points of view and express their overwhelming sense of conflict.

Having first established herself as a genuinely sincere leader with
a strong commitment to assume responsibility for homeless children

and their families, Carole's second strategy was to empower her teachers via "problem ownership" by appealing to their sense of goodness, righteousness, and obligation.

THE ISSUE OF PROBLEM OWNERSHIP

Carole was not interested in assigning blame for the social and economic anguish surrounding and infiltrating B.F. Day. Her desire was to empower teachers with the belief that they could make a difference in at least one child's life and that they were free to make sensible decisions in the light of a shared morality. In one teacher's words:

> I make educational and disciplinary decisions all day long. Every one of them is based on a sound understanding of who my kids are as well as the positive or negative impact I may have upon each of them.... You have to understand the pain these children experience every day of their lives. Only then do you fully realize the need for a different kind of schooling. Some kids are sleeping on mattresses sprawled on a floor. They have no hot-water facilities in their apartments, no heat, no real sense of security. Can you blame them for coming to school with "an attitude"? In all good conscience, I can't. They are innocent human beings who are economically compelled to live amidst an atrocity of circumstances. This school may be their only safe haven.

Carole constantly communicated her sincere belief in the value of socialized education—over breakfast, over lunch, over a microphone in school assemblies—making it clear that the teachers could make all the difference in the world or none at all.

Peter Block (1987) suggests that school efforts to respond to unmet individual and community needs may be maximized if educators seek "an opportunity to support autonomy and to create an organization of [their] own choosing" (p. 97), rather than waiting for the edicts of higher-level school officials:

> Cultures get changed in a thousand small ways, not by dramatic announcements emanating from the boardroom. If we wait until top management gives leadership to the change we want to see, we miss the point. For us to have any hope that our own preferred future will come to pass, we provide the leadership. We hope that the world around us supports our vision, but even if it doesn't, we will act on that vision. Leadership is the process of translating intentions into reality. (pp. 97–98)

In this way, Block asserts, like-minded educators can create critical masses of power at the school building level to bring about improvements in the surrounding community. This appears to be the avenue of thought and action that the principal of B.F. Day pursued.

In order for Carole effectively to enlist those who were to represent and stand by the school's covenant, she would have to educate both white and African-American middle-class teachers about the daily frustrations of ghetto living. Carole's third strategy, therefore, was to heighten their awareness of the world just beyond the school's doors. Teachers were strongly urged to visit shelters, parks, and the temporary homes in which students were residing. Although such journeys were not mandatory, the majority of teachers did in fact accept the responsibility for learning about the surrounding neighborhood. The following comments reflect a growing understanding both from these trips and from conversations with their principal:

TEACHER: Carole constantly reminded us of what life was like in the inner-city ghettos. You know, kids walking through streets strewn with drug vials and liquor bottles, stepping over intoxicated or drug-abused bodies sprawled out across doorways. From the child's point of view, the most successful people in the neighborhood were the pimps and drug pushers. Carole helped many of the teachers see that school was the children's only escape from chaos, defeat, and despair.

When you see the world through Carole's eyes, the word *teacher* takes on a whole new meaning. Children need to know that their teachers care about them, and I'm not talking about their reading and math grades. Those things fall into place when the children have a sense of being nurtured and valued as whole human beings with needs that extend far beyond the acquisition of academic skills.

TEACHER: In the absence of discipline and the traditional "Father Knows Best" role model, boys learn about the rites to manhood on the streets. If a young boy can demonstrate his prowess by fathering a child, breaking the law, or committing a violent act in order to secure a piece of territory in the ghetto, he can gain the respect of his peers. If you are hungry enough for recognition and a sense of belonging, aberrant behavior becomes necessary....

So as far as Carole was concerned, school had to become a safe haven and a model neighborhood. Teachers had to entice children with a sense of nurturance, belonging, and a successful route to adulthood.

Sergiovanni (1984) describes the communication of a vision as "purposing"; it may best be thought of as a process through which the principal signals to others, through his or her actions, what is valued and desired in the way of ideology, goals, and behaviors.

> What the leader stands for and believes about schooling, the place of education in society, how schools should be organized and operated, and how people should be treated comprise the guiding principles which bring integrity and meaning to leadership....
> Purposing breathes life and meaning into the day to day activities of people at work.... Through this process, seemingly ordinary events become meaningful.... It represents as well the rallying point for bringing together all human resources into a common cause.... (p. 108)

One African-American teacher, James Matthews, eloquently depicted the moral and emotional climate fostered by the school principal during and beyond the first year of KOOL-IS as Carole impelled teachers to understand ghetto life by viewing it with their own eyes:

> Carole implored her staff to leave the safety of school turf and cross that fine boundary line which separates school and neighborhood. I suppose it is this same invisible boundary line that separates the teacher from the family life and after-school world of his students. Once you have crossed the line, you are never quite the same as a professional or as a person.... You see, the urban ghetto is full of sights and sounds that just boggle the mind and penetrate the soul. Once you have seen it, you cannot turn your back on it because it continues to influence every step you take.

As more and more teachers visited the homes and shelters of their students, they began to feel the need to do something about this social injustice that inflicts pain and suffering on its innocent victims. Carole was the catalyst that impelled teachers to take a long, hard look, but it was the face-to-face encounters with ghetto reality that formed a bond of morality, of good conscience, of purposeful interaction among the staff.

When the majority of teachers achieved that special bond, taking a personal and professional stand to do something about their students' homelessness, B. F. Day became both a social and an educational service agency.

CHAPTER 4

Social Reconstructionist Theory
in Practice

During the 1980s, major demographic shifts within and among social and economic classes residing in the surrounding community resulted in an increase in homeless students at B. F. Day. The city was in the midst of urban renewal that had caused the demolition of 800 low-income housing units between 1980 and 1988 and would cause 1,200 additional units to be destroyed before the end of 1990. Only 1,000 replacements were slated to be built, and those not until the period from 1991 to 1995.

The change in the social composition of B. F. Day led to a problem-solving orientation on the part of principal and staff in order to cope with concomitant factors affecting some of the developmental, socialization, and learning patterns among the students. It led as well to Carole's growing concern that her students have housing, food, and clothing—prerequisites to learning anything in the classroom. But how was she to obtain these essentials for them when the social service bureaucracy had failed?

Carole thought long and hard, trying to define the gap between where the school's parent community was and where it might be. In order successfully to incorporate social purposes into her mission, she set out to reconstruct the philosophy of the school. As she did this, she and her staff faced the question of whether a school and a community should make an ethical commitment to help individuals actively create and shape their world.

In the course of Carole's exploration of a new direction for her school and its parent community, a model program emerged called KOOL-IS: Kids Organized On Learning In School. Students and their families began to talk to administrators and staff at B. F. Day about their daily social life and problems after 3 P.M., and the school was better able

Gary Jennings, special education teacher: "These children do not have a home life. We are their family. We have to treat them as ours."

to provide necessary basic services so that children could attend school ready and able to concentrate and learn.

KOOL-IS provides funding, as well as human capital in the form of volunteers from local businesses, churches, and all walks of life, to secure permanent housing, furnishings, dishes, pots and pans, bedding, clothing, and food to needy school families. Case managers follow leads to permanent housing sites, and volunteers pick up and transport whatever is needed to create a place called "home." United Way and McKinney Act funds are the primary monetary sources, but it appears to be the local neighborhood people and school staff who provide the essential resources of labor and love that are at the heart of the program. In short, KOOL-IS is an interactive network comprising the principal, the teachers, a local social service agency, a university child study team, neighborhood and corporate volunteers, and government, foundation, and corporate funding, all focused on addressing the needs of homeless children and their families.

B. F. Day's interactive network extends outside its walls. Ordinary people with ordinary knowledge are the natural resources of this community; the school serves as a center for information and social collaboration. By sharing the same vision, both community and school share the process of schooling.

ORDINARY PEOPLE PLAYING OUT A REAL-LIFE DRAMA

Given an educational system in which schools rarely act as agents of social change, I questioned how one school could successfully challenge traditional bureaucratic barriers, fusing the resources of family, community, and formal education. I found within the story of B. F. Day Elementary School an inspirational subplot about ordinary people attempting to fight a wearisome battle against human misery, bureaucratic blinders, and an impersonalized and fragmented social service system.

The recollections of small children and their overwhelmed mothers are powerfully engaging, as are the voices of warm and dedicated professionals who chose to fly in the face of prevailing societal and bureaucratic pressures in order to connect with families in crisis. The professionals I encountered were not superhuman, nor were the students and parents extraordinary. Rather, submerged in poverty, social dislocation, and psychological defeat, these were ordinary children and their mothers, playing out a real-life drama of enduring adversity and crippling despair with little more demulcent support than their unwavering faith in their neighborhood school. But the volunteers, each one only as powerful and proficient as any other ordinary person, appeared to find extraordinary strength and ability in their genuine teamwork and moral commitment to a vision of how different the children's lives might be.

Currently, within the setting and local surround of this central school base, which is often referred to as the "Day Family School," multiply disadvantaged children and adults appear to be thriving, in response to a spectrum of extremely individualized reach-out-and-follow-up social services.

CONTEMPORARY SOCIAL RECONSTRUCTIONISTS

In considering the set of beliefs that facilitated the transformation of the school, I analyzed the animated and emotional statements obtained during formal and informal interviews in the light of social reconstructionist theory.

Encapsulated in a utopian ideology, reconstructionism is founded on the premise that schools must have a culturally enabling and regenerative function that affords a means for reshaping the future. In order to end a mindless state of acquiescence to chronic social ills, "social reconstructionism demands that schools recognize and respond to their role as a bridge between what is and what might be, between the real and the ideal" (Eisner & Vallance, 1974, p. 11).

To counteract the suppressive conditions of urban anonymity, teachers, students, and parents must act concertedly to launch viable alternatives for the collective rebuilding of the community. It is the contention of past and present-day social reconstructionists that social fragmentation and isolation, group conflict, disregard for human dignity, and a barrenness in future hopes and dreams cannot be left outside the classroom door. If these issues are not addressed, formal education will be rendered virtually meaningless in promoting the welfare of the masses within a democracy (Addams, 1910; Goodlad, 1984).

At B. F. Day, it became clear that the pockets of economic collapse and human suffering in the surrounding neighborhood served as catalysts to generate ethical commitment and responsiveness by numerous individuals who actively addressed the school as the place "where it all comes together." Principal, teachers, and neighborhood residents, and agencies fused social and economic resources with the resources of formal education in order to better the human condition. To this extent, the values, beliefs, and attitudes of social reconstructionist philosophy can be seen at work in the path this school chose to follow.

A self-proclaimed social reconstructionist in theory and in practice, principal Carole Williams affirmed her strong belief in the school as a vital lever of social reform as she articulated her school's guiding principles:

> As a black woman who has seen more pain in the faces of neglected and abused children than I can bear to think about, I believe there is no purpose to schooling if it does not focus upon and strongly affect the cold, stark, everyday realities of little human beings ensnared in a poverty from which there is an obscured chance of escape.
>
> As the principal of B. F. Day, I choose not to be concerned with the established societal standards and bureaucratic dictates of "doing things right." Rather, I choose to illuminate a compelling direction of "doing the right thing." I want teachers who are willing to go the 200 yards when it comes to letting children know we will never give up on them. If that translates into hugging and holding a psychologically beaten child, if it means walking down the street and buying him a hamburger, or washing that child's face and combing his hair—whatever—I expect it.
>
> To those who say, "Schools are for educating children," I say, "We can educate children as to the meaning of love, trust, respect, and hope, or we can educate them as to the meaning of desperate cries that fall upon deaf ears and a disregard for human pain."...
>
> There is no magic at B.F. Day. Any school can fulfill the unmet needs of children. All you need is a sense of purpose, a sense of direction, a passionate belief that you can make a difference in the life of an innocent child. If you accept nothing short of that, then your personal integrity and uncompromising sentiments will empower you to excel and breathe life into your daily, moment-to-moment decisions and actions within and beyond the school setting.

Providing physical and psychological access to a warm and intimate school environment, in which children and mothers can and do feel truly respected and cared about, seems to be the essential foundation supporting the effective intervention offered by B. F. Day.

Janet Jones Preston, B. F. Day's family support worker since September 1988, expressed her strong conviction that "one must do what is right" by whatever means necessary:

> If an impoverished or homeless child has head lice and you send him back to his mother, you may not see him again for a month. Often, the mother just does not have the money to purchase the

necessary medication, and so the problem persists. The alternative is simply to put on a pair of surgical gloves and apply the necessary medication directly to the child's head in the privacy of the nurse's office. The health problem is resolved and the child may return to class.

You may ask, "Why should I engage in the personal hygiene of a child that is not mine?" I ask you, "Why should I not engage in such a simple task when a little bit of shampoo can wash away a child's sense of shame?"

Families that are living in dilapidated housing or shelters or garages or abandoned buildings do not have access to the essential necessities that afford personal hygiene. Many of our children live in places that don't provide a shower or warm water. These children do not have access to soap or shampoo or combs and brushes—all the things most of us take for granted. In the nurse's office, we have a shower and a washing machine, and yes, we use them every day.

In most schools across this country, the principal won't get his or her hands dirty. That legitimizes every teacher, every paraprofessional, every one on staff to keep their hands clean as well. When you work in a school such as B. F. Day, and you see a principal bend down and clean the scuff marks off a child's shoes or wipe a child's runny nose and wash his face, then it raises your level of consciousness and gives you the license and the inspiration to dirty your own hands.

People who work with children every day must assume ownership of those problems that precede and follow school hours. If "it is not my job," tell me, *whose job is it?*

This deep-rooted sense of morality and purpose permeated the emotional climate of B. F. Day. The details of how and why this moral commitment to a group of homeless children came about slowly unfolded as each individual told his or her unique story.

IN THE BEGINNING ...

Many of the teachers recollected the strong sense of individual and collective inadequacy in dealing with the challenges presented by homeless students. "The greatest challenge was trying not to blame the kids or their families for having fallen through the cracks of society," stated one teacher. She continued:

In many ways, we refused to acknowledge our own prejudice and bias regarding the homeless population. We had little understanding of their plight. Sometimes it's easier to look away from a situation than to see it up close—real close.

One weekend, I visited an emergency shelter. It looked like an army barracks, only the occupants in each bed weren't soldiers. I mean, this wasn't some kind of comfortable bed-and-breakfast lodging, as I had imagined. There were these sad little faces and these scrawny little bodies huddled together maybe to keep safe, maybe to keep warm....

I spotted one of my students. I knew she would be there, only she looked rather different than the rambunctious 6-year-old kid who typically knocked over someone else's chair or books each day. At the shelter, Jewel looked incapable of knocking over a fly. She had obviously wet her pants. She was holding onto this ripped baby blanket and was sucking all four fingers. She looked like this little ragamuffin that desperately needed to be cared for.

I walked up to her and said the usual "Hi." I expected her to say what she usually did in school: "Get outta my face." But she didn't say that at all. That scrawny little girl looked up at me with those sad eyes of hers and asked if I could take her to school. Can you imagine?... This child who acted like hell on wheels five days a week asked if I could take her to school....

When she actually returned that Monday morning, I hugged her. Do you know what she said? "Get outta my face." Yeah, just like that: "Get outta my face." I think I finally understood Jewel's problem. As one of my colleagues put it, "Jewel has been so busy worrying about minor things like food, shelter, and clothing—let alone a little love and maternal nurturance—that she hasn't had time to learn the social graces."

I love that child. She has come a long way since I began to look at life from her point of view.

Some teachers' recollections focused on the disharmony between homeless children and children with homes. "Yeah, you could feel the discrimination and the tension between the students. Homeless students were often called 'shelter rats' or even worse: 'garbage,' 'recycled trash,' 'losers.'"

In attempting to describe a typical day before KOOL-IS was established, most teachers focused on classroom discord and chaos. One novice teacher expressed her sentiments in this way:

When you wake up in the morning and dread going to work, you begin to wonder why you chose to become a teacher in the first place. I never expected the discipline problems to be of the magnitude they were. After a while, I assumed the role of a police officer, and if I could maintain some semblance of control in the classroom, I considered it a successful day....

You asked about the modifications in curriculum prior to KOOL-IS. There were no modifications because there was no curriculum. Teaching subject matter was not on the agenda; keeping kids from hurting each other took priority.

Another teacher expressed her sentiments in this way:

The homeless kids were hurting, the kids with homes were hurting, the teachers were hurting. We needed help. The question was where to find it.

Janet Jones Preston, described the social climate of the school prior to the initiation of KOOL-IS, and the life circumstances of the homeless child:

When I initially arrived at B. F. Day [in 1988], I experienced the overall school climate as one of hysteria. As the only family support worker appointed to this site, I felt the pressures one might feel in an environment similar to that of a crisis clinic. The job was very stressful that first year because I was not working from a specified job outline but rather from a sense of instinct as to which issues needed to be addressed and in what priority....

People who are homeless are often caught up in a vicious cycle. They are compelled to pay for emergency housing; it is one of the traps of homelessness. They end up using so much of their income to pay for a temporary shelter that they can't save the necessary money for a permanent residence.

If a family does not have cooking utensils or is not permitted to heat food in their room, they have no choice but to eat out a great deal of the time, and that is an expense. It is impossible for such a family to eat economically; the mother does not have the option of cooking a big pot of pasta or vegetables or rice.... The inability to save money is part of a cycle and a set of circumstances where the options are few and the daily living expenses are great....

Then there is the issue of parent involvement in their child's education. A mother living in a shelter may be an hour or more from the school.... If she were to travel by public transportation, she might have to transfer from bus to bus several times. Assuming that the mother had the necessary bus fare, she would most likely have other infants and preschoolers accompanying her on this trip. Such a journey may appear insurmountable to an already overwhelmed and emotionally exhausted single parent.

As for the poorly nourished and often sleepy children who survive the long and often uncomfortable bus ride to school each day, is it any wonder that they are unable to concentrate on their work? Is it any wonder that they are distractable, irascible, angry, or depressed?...

Many of these children have been referred to as "shelter rats" by their classmates. If such children do not demonstrate a readiness to learn, is it ethically right to place blame upon them and their families for being victims of an economic and social system that does not work? For some, it is easier to blame the victim than to seek the solution to a shameful set of circumstances.

The principal of B. F. Day chose to search for that solution as she pursued the initiation and implementation of KOOL-IS. Recalling the tension between the gifted program and the rest of B. F. Day, Carole remarked that she had learned two important lessons by observing Orca's parents and teachers:

First, I frequently thought to myself that while the Orca teachers were supporting their students by projecting a positive image to them, we were reinforcing the homeless children's internal feelings that they were not worthy. Orca parents and teachers believed in their children. They conveyed their faith to their children. They never said anything bad about their kids. Ever. Second, the teachers and the parents banded together. They supported each other, they acted as advocates for each other and their children, and they would not let bureaucracy get in the way of what was best for their children.

Gary Jennings, a special education teacher, commented on the way Carole translated this understanding into action:

Carole made it clear to all of the teachers: "These children do not have a home life. We are their family. We have to treat them as ours."

In so saying, Carole turned the rocky impasses of these children's lives into climbable footholds that marked the beginning of their ascent from social inequalities, class barriers, and despair. The principal and staff of B. F. Day were well on the way to practicing social reconstructionism at its best.

CHAPTER 5

The Power
of Teacher Commitment

In 1831, the French philosopher Victor Cousin proclaimed, "As is the teacher, so is the school." The power of teachers to define a school has since been demonstrated in the work of Little (1982), Hargreaves (1989), and many others. Key to the creation of a shared reality between school and community is the cultural ethos, commitment, and sense of efficacy felt by the teachers. This sense of efficacy in helping small children grow and succeed and the sense of pride in doing what is morally right are powerful motivations for teachers to engage in and pursue meaningful change (Cooper, 1988; Deci, 1976; McLaughlin & Pfeifer, 1988). As Fullan (1982) wrote: "Educational change depends on what teachers do and think—it's as simple and as complex as that" (p. 107).

One of the most acclaimed sociological studies of what teachers think and feel was published by Dan Lortie (1975). Among the many crucial revelations uncovered in his study were two of particular relevance to the ideas presented in this book. In response to a multiple-choice question designed to identify "sources of professional satisfaction and encouragement," 86% of the respondents in his study chose "psychic rewards" as the modal answer—"the times I know I have 'reached' a student or group of students and they have learned." Without doubt, "psychic rewards" and teacher commitment feed on each other, increasing the teachers' motivation to channel energy toward student growth (p. 104).

The second revelation was that 64% of the elementary school teachers in the study focused their thoughts of personal and professional pride around "striking success with one student" (p. 121). Their recollections often featured students who were stigmatized due to severe personal problems or social dislocation. In these cases, in spite of a "dismal beginning, the teacher's persistence in the face of unfavorable prospects" led to a restoration of faith on the part of both adult and child (p. 121).

James Matthews, Grade 3/4 teacher: "The urban ghetto is full of sights and sounds that just boggle the mind and penetrate the soul. Once you have seen it, you cannot turn your back on it."

The values and personal commitments reflected in such stories may be particularly influential in the construction and implementation of school programs that focus on homeless students and their plight. The goal of "righting social wrongs" may very well alter the purpose of schooling and create a climate of mutual respect, bonding, and shared expectations among teachers, students, and parents. As Peters and Waterman (1982) reaffirmed: "Nothing is more enticing than the feeling of being needed, which is the magic that produces high expectations" (p. 240).

To this end, the teacher plays a fateful role, one that establishes a social and psychological sense of the school's orientation, in the implementation of such a program as KOOL-IS. One of the teachers at B. F. Day had this to say:

> It's not difficult to become jaded—you know, to have a suspicious attitude or a hardened outlook. After 12 years of teaching hardcore kids, you begin to question why you ever became a teacher in the first place. I mean you enter the profession with grand ideas of changing the world. It doesn't take more than the first six months to shake you up a bit.... These kids don't want to learn, they want to be obnoxious and wild and outright antisocial.
>
> Then one day, you come upon a kid who is really hurting, and you reach out to him, and to your surprise the child reaches back. You start to think, "Just maybe I can turn things around for this child." And one day, you succeed, and then you remember why you wanted to become a teacher in the first place.

In certain instances, it was a child who reached out first. Jo Daly, the music teacher, arrived at B. F. Day shortly after Carole. Jo is a vibrant teacher, an academic innovator who created totally new and multiethnic programs specifically for the children of B. F. Day. But her first memories of the school were of "psychologists trying to put Band-Aids on peoples' minds." Children were throwing chairs around in the music room. She was hit in the face by a hardball in her own room when two children were fighting. Jo remembered going, overwhelmed, to Carole and hearing Carole tell her, "You've got to stretch yourself farther than you ever have before. You can do it. I know you can." She felt inspired, but her classroom remained chaotic.

Then, several weeks later, a little girl from Cambodia put her mouth to Jo's ear and said, "I love you, Jo Daly." And it was at that moment, according to Jo, "that I realized that as a teacher, the love that I felt for each child had to be unconditional. That this child was accepting me just as I was. That was a major turning point for me."

As for students, commitment and the desire to learn are clearly and directly affected by teacher expectations, the patience and caring of the teacher, and the degree of communication that motivates and engages students in the learning process (Ashton & Webb, 1986; Firestone & Rosenblum, 1988; Mortimore, Sammons, Stoll, Lewis, & Ecob, 1988; Rosenholtz, 1989). As Comer (1980) so eloquently remarked, "Learning the meaning of 'A' has as much significance to children as learning the meaning of *, a nonsense symbol, has to us. Children only learn 'A', how and when to use it, because important people want them to do so" (p. 33).

To be sure, meaningful social interaction is a precursor to meaningful academic learning. Successful implementation of any change, whether academic or social in nature, is just as dependent on what the student thinks and feels as it is on what the teacher thinks and feels. One cannot lecture or demand change on the part of a student any more than one can lecture or demand change on the part of a teacher. The importance of a healthy channel of communication and exchange of emotion between teacher and student should not be underestimated.

COLLEGIAL AND COLLABORATIVE EXCHANGE

Numerous studies over the past 20 years (Ashton & Webb, 1986; Goodlad, 1984; King, Warren, & Peart, 1988; Lortie, 1975; Rosenholtz, 1989; Wigginton, 1986) corroborate teachers' reports of the following problems that impede change:

- Teacher isolationism
- Little if any real collaboration between principal and staff
- Autonomous and idiosyncratic resolution of classroom problems related to discipline and/or instruction
- Infrequent sense of efficacy
- Perennial frustration with lack of time, lack of administrative support, and lack of parental interaction
- Little sense of shared community, often accompanied by negative attention to schoolwide goals
- Poor mobilization of resources in agreed-upon directions in the absence of shared governance
- Abundant cynicism regarding past and future school reforms

A precondition for engaging in any successful change effort is a better understanding of the process as it is experienced by the classroom teacher. Isolation versus collegiality provides perhaps the best starting point for considering what works for the teacher (Fullan, 1991). Since teachers spend most of their time physically and emotionally isolated from their colleagues, each is compelled to struggle privately with frustration, disillusionment, and uncertainty. There is little sense of a common mission. Above all, there is a lack of collegiality and mutual networking. According to McLaughlin and Yee (1988): "In schools with low levels of collegial exchange, it is difficult to create shared norms or to build a sense of common purpose for [school] improvement" (p. 35).

But when professional isolation of teachers is reduced, the door is opened to the sharing of a common language, successful practices, and a vision of what school life could be like, as well as to joint support, trust, and encouragement (Fullan, 1991; Hargreaves, 1989). Moreover, when teachers collaborate, there is an increase in enthusiasm and energy along with a greater sense of efficacy (Cohen, 1988; Rosenholtz, 1989).

Teachers will collaborate constructively with administrators in designing and adopting new ways to improve school life when they have the opportunity to interact within a climate that is "learning enriched" (Rosenholtz, 1986) and that encourages "problem-solving rather than problem-hiding" (McLaughlin & Yee, 1988):

> A problem-solving environment is characterized by a strong sense of group purpose that encourages teachers to reflect on their practice and explore ways to improve it on an ongoing, rather than episodic, basis. It is an environment in which it is safe to be candid and to take the risks inherent in trying out new ideas or unfamiliar practices.
>
> Conversely, in problem-hiding environments, teachers hide their problems and then hide the fact that they are hiding problems. (p. 36)

Finally, collaborative environments provide adequate resources and the essential and continuous support of external consultants as well as a reasonable timeline to work through the subjective meaning of each small step in the change process.

FINDING TIME TO WORK TOGETHER AT B. F. DAY

To make time for a collegial dialogue regarding the school's problems and the possibilities embodied in KOOL-IS, Carole created free periods of up to one hour each day for groups of six to eight teachers at a time. To allow for each teacher's release time from classroom work, she drew upon district funds that were awarded to the school to implement an African Focus Arts Project. Artists, musicians, and artisans were invited to teach and perform at the school, and groups of children within specific grade levels would assemble and receive instruction while classroom teachers collaborated on an array of pressing issues.

In this way, Carole could accomplish two goals simultaneously: The entire student body would be exposed to a whole new world of art and music, while the teachers received work time set aside for planning academic strategies. Drawing on grant money, the principal wasted no time in hiring up to six people at any given time, including those in the community who knew and wished to recount African cultural values and folktales with morals, demonstrate clothes-making techniques, and disclose what Carole called "secret culinary delights." Carole worked closely with her staff to create two mentor positions designed to organize collaboration. Those teachers selected to be team leaders were paid by private donations from supportive community businesses. As word spread about the program, more and more people became its allies.

The traditional school day was further restructured by requiring teachers to arrive 15 minutes earlier each day. The earlier starting time meant that district time requirements for teacher/classroom contact hours were fulfilled earlier in the month, and Carole was able to set aside two whole days a month for teacher workshops in the legal absence of students. The school district and the State Department of Education approved the change, and the bus companies cooperated. Not all teachers and parents were content with this arrangement, but little choice was offered. To those who saw changes in traditional scheduling as unjust and wished to dispute the matter, Carole merely responded, "No one ever said life was fair. Why even our homeless kids know that!"

In spite of "widespread dissatisfaction with one scheduling detail or another," teachers began to benefit from being required to spend time together. "There were newly formed buddy systems and the discovery of a kindred soul," stated one teacher.

The how-to concerns of dealing with specific situations—the withdrawn child, the acting-out child, the absentee parent, the hostile parent—were tossed around, deliberated, and decided on during informal meetings as well as set-aside times, according to several teachers. As the staff worked through project precepts and "learning" became a process of "doing," each teacher was able to determine whether the reconstructionist ideology underlying the KOOL-IS model was workable at the level of his or her own classroom.

POWER SHARING

The school principal is perhaps the most powerful figure in establishing and directing the social realities within and around any one educational setting and its surrounding parent community. He or she is often the key negotiator among staff, neighborhood, and "the system" (Blumberg

& Greenfield, 1981; Goodlad, 1987; Smith & Andrews, 1989; Wilson & Corcoran, 1988).

Louis and Miles (1990) found that leaders in successful schools fostered power sharing by delegating authority to hierarchical steering groups consisting of teachers, parents, and students, while maintaining an active liaison with the groups. Many researchers have shown that the additional leadership that emanates from the school staff and engaged community is of equal significance to that provided by the principal (Ascher, 1988; Barth, 1990; Comer, 1980; Fine, 1993; Firestone & Rosenblum, 1988; Lieberman & Miller, 1986; Mortimore et al., 1988).

Sergiovanni (1991) has called this characteristic of the effective school "leadership density" and has discussed it in this way:

> Leadership density refers to the total leadership available from teachers, support staff, parents, and others on behalf of the school's work. Of course, the principal plays a key role in building and maintaining leadership density. In this sense, principal leadership can be understood as an enabling process.
>
> Principals practice enabling leadership when they help teachers, students, and staff to function better on behalf of the school and its purposes, to engage more effectively in the work and play of the school, and to promote the achievement of the school's objectives. It is crucial to build up the leadership capacity of others, and in this sense the principal is a leader of leaders. (p. 76)

As the key negotiator, the principal sincerely endorses power sharing between the teachers and the families of the children they teach. This is critical, considering the "authentic possibility that borders which now separate the school from its parental clientele may finally be crossed without alarm, and that the 'crossing' may take place in both directions" (Kozol, 1985, p. 216).

Key to the development of strong ties among school, family, and neighborhood is the true concern of the principal and the ability of teachers to break the barriers of privatism and isolationism in reaching out to colleagues as well as parents and community members.

CHAPTER 6

Affiliations with Community, University, and Corporations

Even working in collaboration, the principal and teachers cannot by themselves generate and control every aspect of a school that is transforming itself into both a social and educational service agency. Carole's next step, therefore, was to reach out to the community for support and advice. By February 1989, Carole had found a local social service agency affiliate that could help her school develop a deeper relationship with the community and could also serve as a recipient of grant money from private foundations and corporations. Carole's first and perhaps most significant contact was Joe Garcia, who at that time was the director of the Atlantic Street Center, a local mission agency related to the United Methodist Church. The center, which was founded in 1908 and is Seattle's oldest settlement house, describes itself as "a refuge for adults, children, youth, and families," with programs targeting "Seattle's low-income and minority population, using a multilingual/multicultural approach" to meet peoples' basic needs and help them lead a "more gratifying and empowered life."

THE RIGHT SOCIAL WORK CONSULTANT

A Vietnam veteran, former migrant worker, and graduate of Yale University, Joe Garcia had established a reputation as a community organizer and social activist specializing in prevention and intervention strategies for at-risk students. He was well known to Collin Williams, Carole's husband, who at that time was Assistant Superintendent of At-Risk and Multicultural Programs of the Seattle School District. Well aware of the crisis at B.F. Day, Collin believed that Joe could be of great help to Carole. After spending a number of days at the school at Carole's

Lory Misel (l.), a clinical social worker, and Barbara Endicott (r.), an executive volunteer from Boeing, joined forces with Carole Williams to establish the first building-based management team in Seattle.

invitation, Joe affirmed her view that issues of homelessness pervaded school life and that the lack of a home/school connection had a negative impact on student/teacher relationships. Both Carole and Joe agreed that one could not separate the realities of school and home life; it was this firm belief that eventually developed into KOOL-IS.

An article published in the *Seattle Times* on May 20, 1989—a portion of which follows—was brought to my attention by one of the teachers at B. F. Day in response to my question: "Who is Joe Garcia? Do you think he was the 'right' man for the job?" Attached to the article was a brief note from the teacher that simply said, "Who is Joe Garcia? He is a lone visionary to be respected and admired."

Youth Advocate Fasts for Children

Joe Garcia, the outspoken executive director of the Atlantic Street Center, has begun a hunger "Fast for Kids," intending to abstain from everything but water until June 7.... The fast is in support of efforts by public officials to negotiate a truce among teen-age gangs and to dramatize Garcia's call for 300 adults to commit four to six hours a week for a year as counselors for inner-city poor children.

Garcia is inviting all area citizens to join him in fasting one day between now and June 7 "as an expression of concern, commitment and love for the area's poor children." Garcia chose June 7 as a day of focus because that is the day Mayor Charles Royer is scheduled to open the new six million dollar elephant house at the Woodland Park Zoo. "The elephant house is a symbol of how a community in a short period of time can raise enough [money] to feed, care for and shelter elephants," Garcia said. "What I'm saying is we ought to do equally as much for the poor kids in this city....

"That's how we are going to save our kids. We're not going to do it with more police action and more signs saying that Seattle's a 'Kid's Place'. It's going to take people working with people." (Angelos, 1989, p. A12)

The teacher who had forwarded the article later said, "There is political rhetoric and plenty of it.... But then there is social action, the kind that has an almost magnetic quality: 'Follow me and together we can make a difference'. That's what Joe Garcia is all about."

Joe is a mover and a shaker. His passionate convictions were evident even in our informal conversation:

We spend billions of dollars on our freeways, our aquariums, our zoos, our brand-new underground bus tunnel.... Why do we not attend as well to our children, the harvest of our society, ravaged by the brutal winds of economic and social turbulence?...

Policy makers are too often caught up in "the magnitude of the problem," "the statistical analysis of the problem," and "the need to do a study of a previous study of the problem." Resourceful people, on the other hand, do not require the accumulation of faceless statistics. They are able to place their trust in community and neighborhood counselors, educators, clergy, and leaders who have sighted a social problem and are expressing a need for immediate intervention....

Our neighborhoods are full of resourceful people. There is the real estate agent who has a knack for finding the most affordable housing in the best areas. There is the carpenter or construction worker who can renovate a tenement apartment over the course of a weekend. There is the dentist who will give freely of his time and expertise in examining the teeth and gums of kids living in an inner-city ghetto and surviving on junk food....

Once upon a time, in pre-1940 America, we didn't have an impersonalized and totally fragmented bureaucracy.... Once upon a time, we had a pretty unsophisticated but effective way of taking care of ourselves and our neighbors. It was called communication, compassion, and caring.

As government became more of the solution and encroached all the way into our small neighborhoods, it took away the little man's responsibility to be his brother's keeper. Unfortunately, the little man knew more about his brother, his friend's family, and his neighbor's children than any bureaucracy ever could.

We have got to become our brother's keeper again, and we can do it if we form links between resourceful people so they are part of a collaborative partnership that provides comprehensive care on a small-scale and extremely personalized basis. We need to reinstate the kind of close-knit interactions among neighborhood authority figures that delineate a sense of community and a sense of belonging.

When you open up opportunities for resourceful people within the surrounding community to work in collaboration with teachers, then those teachers can remove the weight of the dozen hats they must wear in the classroom each day. As each resourceful person assumes the weight of one of those hats, the teacher is provided the emotional support she requires in order to be the best teacher she can be.

It is this interactive network of people in combination with an effective school leader called a principal that are the key ingredients to having teachers become receptive and highly functional in a school that serves as both a social service and educational institution.

Both Carole and Joe agreed that there were few parts of the community they could *not* see as having a role to play in the school's transformation. The pieces of this puzzle were there waiting to be positioned; the task was to connect the pieces and then keep them in place.

"CONNECTED" VOLUNTEERS

Bev Parker, an active community volunteer, was soon to become the central linking piece between the educators at B. F. Day and a whole crew of volunteers to be recruited from the Mercer Island United Methodist Church. Bev, the center of the volunteer component of KOOL-IS, may be described as an affluent citizen very much involved in diverse community agencies and social service affairs. She is a knowledgeable individual of gentle demeanor and diplomatic, but determined, character. Her silver-gray hair, blue eyes, soft smile, and mesmerizing voice create an aura that seems to capture and engage the hearts and minds of those drawn to her.

Bev was described by Carole Williams as "the network leader without whom the outcome of collaborative efforts that first critical year might have been quite different." Asked to respond to Carole's comment, Bev said:

> In some way, Carole Williams, Robert Mann [the KOOL-IS case manager], and I had become a self-appointed core group, and so we felt an obligation to make KOOL-IS work. Each of us sensed the plethora of potential resources intrinsic in a network concept of volunteers. If we could connect individuals to the school building, we could expand our resources in unquantifiable ways....
>
> When Joe Garcia called and requested my help with the KOOL-IS program, we agreed on the necessity for an individualized assessment.... The success of the program is due to the fact that there is a filling in here where somebody needs this, and a filling in there where somebody needs that.
>
> We were never really organized as some social service agencies are, and maybe that is why things get done. We discover a need, and we fill it. We don't fill out requisition forms or applications for required goods. We simply reach out to other human resources who can provide us with those necessities which fill a basic human need such as food, clothing, shelter, and medical care.
>
> The disparity between what we need and what we can get is only as great or small as the unnecessary limitations we impose

upon ourselves. Where there is an imagination, there is a way. If we are going to rebuild our communities, we are going to have to look more deeply into ourselves, our neighbors, and our religious beliefs and values.

Pastor Jack Olive of the Mercer Island United Methodist Church, an extremely active participant in the volunteer network, eloquently captured both the essence of Bev and the way KOOL-IS works on the personal level:

> When a parishioner named Bev Parker comes to church on a Sunday morning with photographs and stories of homeless children and their families, our parish can see and hear the psychological defeat that abounds in [their] lives.... The photographs and stories bring these despairing people to life, for they are no longer faceless drifters without names whom we pass by on the street each and every day....
>
> Oh, I cannot tell you how many parishioners express a desire to help and carry through in all sorts of ways. People seem most capable of responding to a specific need, a specific face, a specific situation. We do best when we attempt to affect one life at a time—far better than when we attempt to take on the social issues of an entire faceless and nameless society.

It was in this way that the Mercer Island United Methodist Church provided at least a dozen committed volunteers who assisted in moving and settling families into affordable housing by picking up and transporting used furniture, dishes, pots and pans, bedding, and the like. They also worked individually with mothers who needed assistance in maintaining a household, budgeting a fixed income, or cooking nutritional meals. Some volunteers provided car rides for parents and children in need of medical care or social service intervention.

The church became perhaps the strongest agency affiliation that could serve as a point from which to begin the process of interconnection among school, family, and community. The individuals in this collaborative chain of genuinely committed volunteers strategically mobilized necessary actions and services to meet the most basic needs of individual families. And, like all chains, each link's motions naturally sent vibrations to all the others. Each individual's actions—as intangible as an exchange of sincere concern, trust, and respect or as concrete as a car ride to the supermarket, laundromat, or pharmacy—reinforced those of others.

By spring 1990 the vibrations were being felt by other churches and businesses in the neighborhood. The 45th Street Clinic sent a physician's assistant each Monday morning to B. F. Day to examine the children, immunize them, and write necessary prescriptions. A local dentist provided free examinations and treatment for several dozen children. Preston's Studio One gave hundreds of free haircuts. The Woodland Park Zoo donated 44 passes for homeless students and their classmates. Even when the donations seemed humble, their impact on the school volunteers and the needy families who received them was tremendous. One local Baptist church gave 200 pairs of socks; another church gave 35 sets of mittens, hats, and scarves; Wallingford United Methodist Church gave 35 book bags packed with school supplies; and Queen Anne Baptist Church provided space to sort out all incoming clothing donations. Volunteers began to collect staple supplies—shampoo, toothbrushes, Kleenex, sanitary napkins—each small donation extremely useful to its final recipient and enriching to the life of each person who handed it on. In the light of this emerging sense of purpose, the volunteers rejoiced. "We are often bankrupt in the caring department," Bev said, "but today we are spiritual millionaires."

One of the most useful donations to the school came from Church Women United's "Dressed for Success" program. The organization's president, Kay Wight, had founded the program after recognizing that the lack of a suitable wardrobe for job hunting is a significant barrier to employment for otherwise qualified women. "Dressed for Success" spent an average of $100 on each mother. Kay Wight assisted students as well as mothers, as she assumed the role of volunteer tutor at B. F. Day.

In an article entitled "Networking for Educational Improvement," Ward and Pascarelli (1987) underscore the nature and value of collaborative networks in operation:

> Effective networks are recognized as self-reliant, involving autonomous individuals or agencies who cohere around shared interests and values, develop resource-sharing solutions to problems, and, in the process, establish new patterns of community and collegiality. Networkers take seriously their roles as scouts, scanners, and matchmakers.
>
> The participants see networking as a serious way of doing business.... Members are committed both to the process of collaborating effectively and to achievement of the prescribed improvements.... [They] identify the very best in human and material resources to solve a given problem. (p. 201)

A viable bridge had been built so that those who were in a secure position and wished to give now had easy access to those who were in desperate need of help. The school became both that bridge and the center of a community in need.

SECURING PARTNERSHIP WITH A LOCAL UNIVERSITY

In a joint decision to employ the resources of a research institute, Carole and Joe contacted Dr. Bill James, a researcher at the Center for the Study and Teaching of At-Risk Students (C-STARS) at the University of Washington. It was their hope that Dr. James might broaden everyone's perspective with a range of psychological and social theories as well as new practices from which the school staff could choose and learn as they attempted to deal with such side effects of childhood homelessness as socialization problems, depression, and aggression. Carole also believed that both formative and summative evaluations of any program design or plan of action would "equip every participant so they might make informed judgments and tailored changes along the way."

Bill James, who joined C-STARS in 1989, recounted his involvement with B. F. Day:

> [C-STARS] already had an evaluation contract with the Seattle Public School District [that] generalized all evaluation efforts ... toward at-risk children, not in any way specific to homeless children....
>
> I was contacted by Carole and Joe.... Carole was extremely distraught because she was faced with youngsters who were exhibiting signs of emotional disturbance due to varied homeless situations....
>
> She made it clear that she was going to make her vision of social justice work one way or the other. Her plan entailed a lot of one-on-one work as she talked with teachers about their frustrations as the population of homeless kids grew. A lot of teachers will not say, "I don't want any homeless kids in my class" or "I'm against having homeless children at this school." Rather, the teaching staff will act out in other ways. They may be uncooperative or indicate issues of prejudice through body language. But Carole's presence and steadfastness seemed to reach out and grasp even the most contrary teachers....
>
> Almost immediately, we began to talk about the need for long-term supports because anything short of that would merely serve as a temporary bandage. Joe came up with the idea of writing a proposal ... to be submitted to the United Way....
>
> Joe and I drafted the original proposal.... [W]e were dealing with a short timeline. We clearly needed to submit a proposal by spring in the hope of obtaining funds for the fall semester. Incidentally, it was Joe who created the acronym KOOL-IS. We needed

a name for the proposal—something catchy—and this was perfect.

In July 1989, the United Way granted a donation of $48,000, which was to be repeated in the future. It included a unique access fund of $12,000. Bill commented:

Unlike the funding for other educational programs designed to assist homeless children, this $12,000 would target issues of housing. It seemed that no matter what you provided—food, clothing, counseling, family support—nothing really changed until the family had a permanent place to live....

Since the Seattle Public School District was not engaged in any specific program for homeless children and youth at that time, they had no idea as to the shift in neighborhood demographics, which directly contributed to an overwhelming number of homeless kids in attendance at B. F. Day. They did approve the proposal forwarded to the ... United Way, but, other than their rubber stamp, involvement on the part of the district was limited.

Bill pointed out, however, that the District was quick to acknowledge the viability of the new program and to move to expand it to other needy families: "You might say that recognition of Carole's successful grass-roots attempt to effect change at the building level ultimately effected change throughout an entire district."

In May 1990, the district expanded the scope of the program to encompass several other school sites. Collin Williams and Bill collaborated on a proposal called the "Effective Schools for Homeless Children and Youth Initiative," and in July 1990, $249,000 was granted from McKinney Act funds for distribution among seven designated homeless sites, including B. F. Day.

In the meantime, Carole, Joe, and Bill continued to talk at length about where the school was and the direction in which it might go with effective leadership, dialogue, and purpose. Joe and Bill assumed the role of external consultants and effective change facilitators, but it was Carole's awakened sense of mission, tenacious expectations, and inspirational images of "how school life ought to be" that became the teachers' common rallying cry and provided the vision toward which the group strove in the weeks and months to follow.

There was a renewal of energy through joint action. Every four months, a formative evaluation was carried out, helping to give the program direction. Summative evaluations were completed at the end of each school year.

OUT OF THE FRYING PAN

When renovations on the school building began in September 1989, the Orca program was moved to Columbia Elementary School. B. F. Day staff and students were displaced to the John Hay School, which was in such bad shape that the move was truly a leap from the frying pan into the fire. Hay was a complex of aged structures: a brick building containing the main office, library, and three classrooms; a free-standing, portable gymnasium; a triple portable containing two classrooms; and a three-story wood building containing four classrooms. None of these buildings connected; teachers and students had to go outside to get from one to the other. To make matters worse 160 first- and second-graders and an additional special education class already attended school at Hay, increasing the total enrollment to 300. Eighty children were designated English-as-second-language students, reading below grade level.

The teachers felt so extremely vulnerable and isolated in the horrible physical plant and overwhelming new academic environment that school life at Hay seemed to them to mimic the chaotic home lives of many of their students. In order to make things work in this stressful time, teachers more than ever needed a sense of strength and a durable infrastructure. The key person who would help provide that infrastructure, develop an independent school-based management team, and promote a strategic plan for effective change was to come from the corporate world.

THE CORPORATE CONNECTION

Barbara Endicott, an executive at Boeing, was required by her management development program to select a volunteer activity. A Caucasian in her early forties, Barbara had then been at Boeing for 17 years. She held M.S. and M.B.A. degrees and had just become adjunct instructor of information systems management at Seattle Pacific University. She had also been a United Way fundraiser through Boeing for many years. Barbara wanted to work where she could make the most difference, so she contacted the superintendent of the school district, William Kendrick, who put her in touch with Carole. Ultimately, Barbara became so involved with the school that, prompted by Carole, William Kendrick approached Boeing and asked for her part-time release for one year. Boeing agreed, in order to help Barbara help B. F. Day establish programs ancillary to KOOL-IS. It was through this set of circumstances that Barbara became a key player in activating proposals and programs that would benefit all children at B. F. Day.

During her initial weeks at the school, Barbara worked closely with Carole to share the management techniques she had learned at Boeing, encouraging her to think of the school as a business that could reach out to other businesses. Together, they worked to empower parents, teachers, and community volunteers through the formation of a building-based management team, one of the first to be formed in the Seattle School District. Essential to the effective functioning of this team was the guidance given by a consulting social worker, Lory Misel (see Chapter 7). The team focused on developing a five-year plan targeting the issues of academic excellence, critical-thinking skills, creative expression, and responsibility to self and community. The plan's vision statement reads:

> We envision B. F. Day to be the school of choice for families within and beyond the neighborhood because of our harmonious educational environment with unlimited resources, where staff, parents, and community serve as mentors and work together with students to develop responsibility to achieve their academic potential and love and respect for themselves, each other, and the world.

Over time, the team began to consider issues pertinent to the school's well-being and discuss sources of financing.

Tutors from High School and College

One of the first issues the team focused on was the development of a tutorial program for the homeless children, who at that point made up 15% of the school's enrollment, as well as for other B. F. Day students. Through a Boeing connection, Barbara contacted the Governor's Leadership Conference, a social service agency with administrative offices at Seattle University that is designated to promote lifetime volunteerism among youth within the community. The Leadership Conference and B. F. Day designed a program that provided 24 high school and college students pretrained to work with underprivileged children; each tutor worked two days a week from 3:30 P.M. to 5:00 P.M. at the school. The program ran for two four-month periods each year, each tutor working for at least one four-month period.

The issue of transportation had to be solved at the outset. The Leadership Conference arranged with Seattle University's Physical Education Department that the tutors would go to the university, where two Physical Education Department vans would take them to B. F. Day and later pick them and the students up to take them home.

Simeon Fields, B. F. Day's new case manager, supervised the tutoring program, and Carole oversaw each child's academic "itinerary": The teachers evaluated each child to be tutored, made up individualized lessons, and explained to the tutors what was to be done and how it was to be done. In cases in which teachers felt that this was beyond the call of duty or had other obligations after school, Carole asked them to select from a standardized reading curriculum appropriate material that followed in a sequence and to create a packet for the child. This one-time effort carried the tutor through the four months.

The children's enthusiasm exceeded even original hopes, and has carried over each year. Even those homeless students whose attendance was poor on other days tended to have a 100% attendance rate on their tutoring days. According to Barbara:

> Tutors themselves became grounded with a sense of responsibility for small children. Many of the tutors were average students—far from A students. As they saw the results of their own efforts, they thought twice about their personal academic and work ethic. They could not tell the children, "Do as I say, not as I do." In return, the children responded overwhelmingly to the teenagers.

Schoolyard Monitors and Other Supports

The second ancillary program the team developed was one to fund and train schoolyard monitors, because of the poorly socialized and sometimes violent behavior of many students. Carole insisted that the monitors be the parents of the homeless children; the parents needed a sense of why they should get up in the morning and go to work, and their children needed role models for working behavior. Through Barbara's efforts, Boeing made the first of several grants: $10,000 for the period from September 1990 through January 1991, some of which was used to buy store credits for food and clothing to be used in exchange for volunteer work done for the school. Parents ride the bus as matrons and work as monitors in the schoolyard, they receive a free lunch, and they are extremely grateful for the opportunity and proud of their abilities and new status.

Boeing also helped Carole put together a parent handbook, provided school stationery, and made up business cards with the school's logo for each individual teacher. According to Barbara, the business cards had the effect of restoring the teachers' sense of themselves as true professionals.

The parents and tutors have taken their roles quite seriously from the start. In the period from September 1989 to January 1990 alone, they donated 1,497 hours of their time in this mutually beneficial program.

Three Meals a Day

The third program that the team created grew from Carole's perception that many children were malnourished and hungry. Bused from far enough away that they missed the school's breakfast time, many children needed food for daytime snacks and food to take home for supper as well. Barbara suggested a corporate partnership with local businesses and proceeded to obtain a grant of $12,000 from Kraft, Inc., for food. She then contacted the Fremont Food Bank, a local agency, which promised to donate food as it was needed.

The Growing Corporate/Scholastic Partnership

Barbara continued to reach out to corporations and schools to enhance the life of B. F. Day. She facilitated grants of $35,000 from the Fremont Commerce Council to establish the Living Classroom, which pays for transportation and admissions on cultural and educational trips; $8,000 from the Windermere Foundation; $5,000 from the Nestle Corporation that the school applied to teacher training in prosocial skills; $5,000 from the Haas Foundation for psychological counseling for students; and $1,000 from the Seattle district of IRS Adopt-a-School Program, which the school used to buy shoes.

Barbara also obtained $3,000 from Egghead Software for computer software to teach the children. Moreover, master's degree students in Barbara's software development and design class at Seattle Pacific University helped build a foundation for computer studies at the school by tutoring teachers at the end of each day. Private donations from corporations and affluent persons in the community provided the computer hardware.

Another computer program currently being pilot-tested in the school, to track the individual performance of students both academically and socially, was developed in a unique way. Barbara's students developed three designs for software systems. One of the students obtained $3,000 from Washington Mutual Savings Bank, his employer, to turn the designs into software that could be used at the school site. The bank, in turn, prompted the Seattle School District to match its donation, and the school district provided $5,000 from its funds for special projects. With this computer software in use, the student no longer will have to reach a point of despair before he or she will be recognized as having emotional, social, or academic problems. The family support worker, the school psychologist, and the teacher will have access to an account of unusual outbursts or a decline in academic performance, which is frequently the tip-off to domestic problems.

Although corporate involvement is virtually absent from most neighborhood schools, B. F. Day was fortunate to receive the support of The Boeing Company, which in 1990 alone made a $9 million "investment" in education throughout the country, of which $2 million went to Kindergarten through Grade 12. Through direct grants, donations of equipment and school supplies, and loaned executives, Boeing has collaborated with numerous schools to identify specific needs and tailor unique programs to match those needs. Surely, they are a pacesetter for other businesses and corporations, both large and small.

CHAPTER 7

A Coalescence of "Significant Adults"

When school resumed in September 1989, Carole and the teachers began to brainstorm about additional ways to change the school climate. They acknowledged a need for at least one strong male figure who might oversee a "time-out" room for the very aggressive and angry boys. Many of these children had slept in the same clothes for days—maybe weeks—at a time. Some had been sleeping on a bench, or in the back of a car, or in somebody's boiler room. The teachers could only begin to imagine the kind of turmoil or havoc that these children experienced before and after school hours. They needed a transition room where they could "unload" all their negative and painful feelings in the presence of a caring and supportive adult, without disrupting an entire classroom.

In the fall of 1989, Robert Mann became the supportive adult overseeing the transition room, assuming the role of primary case manager. A tall, young-looking Caucasian man in his thirties with master's degrees in music and religious studies, Robert has been a teacher, a counselor, and an educative administrator. He has a soft-spoken manner that presents a strong contrast to the more assertive personality of Joe Garcia. Recounting the early stages of KOOL-IS within B. F. Day, he focused first on the immediate need to scale the idealistic down to the realistic because of funding problems:

> The original KOOL-IS model as it appeared on paper and the realities of external funding clashed. The program called for a case manager, at least one counselor, and a special education teacher to oversee the transition room. This room was to be a safe haven for kids lacking that basic sense of security one might generally get from a stable home environment.

Bev Parker, a community volunteer, flanked by Robert Mann (l.), the initial KOOL-IS case manager, and Bill James (r.), a researcher at the University of Washington's C-STARS program.

A child who has spent the night in a shelter or on the street is often in a state of dissonance with himself and the world around him. He may be hungry, exhausted, depressed, or feeling ill. Such a child needs a place to rest, receive some nourishment, and perhaps let out his frustrations on a punching bag or cry in the arms of an accepting adult.

B. F. Day had requested $155,000 from the United Way, which would have covered the salaries for three professionals to man the transition room. The school received a grant of $48,000, which included a housing access fund of $12,000, so Carole had no choice but to hire one individual in the hope that a counselor and teacher would later be assigned by the district office. That never happened, and so you might say I was stretched pretty thin in a number of directions until Bev Parker volunteered her time and extensive efforts.

Bev Parker was a real key figure in terms of opening lines of communication and connecting with the community. She had a way of getting neighborhood people to commit themselves, whether in the form of material donations or in the form of time. A local carpet company donated a beautiful area rug for the transition room. We were able to obtain a sofa and some cozy chairs. We brought in a bunch of soft, stuffed animals so that the children might experience a bit of "home."

In addition to funding problems, there were initial problems with teachers' perceptions of the transition room. According to Robert:

I was concerned that time spent in the transition room did not in any way stigmatize homeless children. I worked closely with the family support worker to ensure that any and all unhappy kids had access to this room, whether homeless or not. We had a variety of activities going on so that this multipurpose room had a positive connotation rather than becoming "a place where the homeless kids go."

Of course, as with any new program, we had several teachers who had their own ideas as to how things should work. They seemed to perceive the transition room as a "dumping ground" for any child they felt unequipped to deal with in the classroom. We had a couple of heated staff meetings about this issue. Although Carole made it clear that the transition room was not to be used for anything and everything perceived as a behavior problem during the course of the day, some teachers continued to define the room as a drop-off point for discipline problems.

From the outset, teacher "overload" and prejudice became issues as well:

> There was the issue of teachers refusing to accept more than a specific quota of kids identified as homeless. I recall one particular incident in which a child and I stood in the doorway of a classroom as a teacher refused to allow us to enter the room. As you might imagine, this teacher made it clear that the child was unwelcome. I wasn't going to push it in front of the child, so I returned to the transition room and worked with the student there.
>
> Later, the teacher, Carole, and I discussed the situation. There were some legitimate issues to be considered in terms of overloading a teacher with "high-needs kids." Many of the children identified as homeless required a great deal of time and patience. Some of the teachers' personalities were such that they could not handle more than one high-needs kid at a time. This was a real issue that had to be dealt with individually as well as with the whole staff.
>
> Then, of course, there was the issue of prejudice, which in some cases manifested itself in the form of scorn and dissension. We were all well aware that if the teachers weren't in touch with their own underlying fears and biases, it would be virtually impossible to tackle the problem of homelessness and its side effects at the school site.
>
> Yeah, it was rough sailing for quite a while there until the direction of the winds began to change.

BUILDING A COALITION WITHIN THE SCHOOL

In order to generate and sustain a viable, working consensus directed toward problem resolution, Carole and Joe focused on a strategy designed to build a communicative and collaborative pattern of interaction among connected, open, and trusting participants. Carole recollected her chain of thoughts:

> If I was going to be an effective leader, I knew I would have to channel and transform a vast number of paralyzing doubts on the part of the teachers into one directive purpose. The question remained as to how to do this. Joe Garcia helped me to see that having a vision of how life might be at B. F. Day was not enough.
>
> In order to induce commitment on the part of the staff, it was crucial that I communicate my strong personal belief in the value of that vision. I had to raise the consciousness of each and

every teacher to a level that would inspire their allegiance, their sense of excitement, as they began to experience and share a common sense of purpose.

I was constantly faced with the question of what thoughts, words, and actions were worthy of focus and emphasis and what issues were to be put aside. I was aware that what I did not say or do might prove as consequential as what I did say or do.

Joe insisted that I maintain an unyielding focus and not lose sight of my vision for B. F. Day. His feeling was that if the going got rough, the staff would drift off course if ever "the leader relinquished the role of navigator." There were definitely moments when I clutched the compass. You ask which way did the arrow face? Toward the nearest land sighting. Even the best of captains get cold feet.

In the most recent literature on the change process inherent in successful educational reform, five major themes are identified that in combination seem to have a crucial impact on organizational arrangements and roles in schools (Marsh, 1988; Rosenholtz, 1989; Wilson & Corcoran, 1988). Louis and Miles (1990) refer to these five themes as vision-building, evolutionary planning and development, initiative-taking and empowerment, resource and assistance mobilization, and problem-coping. This recent reconceptualization of the change process is concisely captured in the findings of a study of successful urban schools conducted by Miles (1987):

> The need for a vision of what the school should look like is affected by two preconditions: the principal must exercise leadership in promoting a vision, but the staff must also be cohesive enough to be willing to buy some shared set of goals. Having a vision leads indirectly to good implementation by creating an enthusiasm that increases willingness and initiative, but also by creating an environment in which a long term vision of the future permits program evolution that is always purposive, but reflects growth of activities rather than limiting implementation. Putting it another way: a good vision provides shared criteria for judging movement. Such evolution also leads, characteristically, to organizational change: new structures and procedures that in turn promote institutionalization. (p. 7)

Coalescence of the entire staff at B. F. Day was a primary foundation for any successful large-scale change. It was crucial that the teachers be part of the solution from the very start. Undoubtedly, infinite variations in life encounters, religion, education, familial values, and beliefs would affect and alter each individual teacher's conception and interpretation of "the problem."

With this in mind, initial meetings involved viewing two intense videos about the effects of prejudice and discrimination. The first video, *Shelter Boy*, portrayed the story of a 12-year-old named Richard Metcalf, who became homeless after a tornado destroyed his home in Omaha, Nebraska. The video focused on the emotional impact this situation had on Richard as he became the victim of classmates who referred to him as "shelter boy" and treated him badly.

The second video, *The Eye of the Storm*, depicted the story of a group of third-graders in Iowa who learned a dramatic lesson in discrimination. The day after Martin Luther King was killed in 1968, Caucasian schoolteacher Jane Elliott decided her Caucasian third-graders should learn how it feels to be on the receiving end of prejudice. In a daring exercise on what was to become "Discrimination Day," Jane Elliott split the class according to eye color, creating a microcosm of society. As described by Peters (1971):

> The rules for the day were enumerated to the growing delight of the brown eyed children and the increasing discomfort of the blue eyed. Brown eyed children could use the drinking fountain in the room as usual. Blue eyed children were to use paper cups. The brown eyed children would have five extra minutes of recess. They would go first to lunch, could choose their lunch-line partners, and could go back for seconds. The blue eyed children could do none of these things....
>
> With the rules established, Jane swung quickly into the day's regular schoolwork. When a brown eyed child stumbled in reading aloud, she helped him. When a blue eyed child stumbled, she shook her head and called on a brown eyed child to read the passage correctly. When a blue eyed boy, tense and nervous, rolled a corner of a page of his reading book into a tight curl as he awaited his turn to read, Jane displayed the book to the class. "Do blue eyed people take care of the things they are given?" she asked....
>
> By the lunch hour,... the blue eyed children were miserable. Their posture, their expressions, their entire attitudes were those of defeat. Their classroom work regressed sharply from that of the day before. Inside of an hour or so, they looked and acted as though they were, in fact, inferior. It was shocking. (p. 22)

It was hoped that a shared viewing would stimulate open dialogue in which each viewer would be inclined to risk expression of his or her own bias. The first video, *Shelter Boy*, triggered rigorous discourse and thought-provoking questions. But it was the second video, *The Eye of the Storm*, that unleashed anger, outrage, and many other emotions that would bring the group together. Robert Mann described his recollection of those first sessions in this way:

These initial meetings were a "teachers only" type of situation. It was clearly an in-house kind of workshop, and there were no visitors or outsiders present. Carole requested that I conduct and direct these sessions.... As a woman of color, Carole felt uncomfortable leading a discussion about racism and prejudice. She could not chance that her position as a black woman principal might impede open dialogue and an honest—really honest—expression of emotion....

It became crystal clear that both racial and economic prejudice on the part of some individual teachers had impacted gravely upon their ability to relate to poor kids in general and poor, minority kids in particular. Discussing *Shelter Boy* gave the teachers an opportunity to openly acknowledge that we all come with prejudice. That's just the way it is.

If you are born in this culture, you are often raised with a value system that has been passed down and sustained through tradition, folktales, and sometimes plain ignorance. This is the context in which we grow up. It's like the air we breathe: It's just there, and it permeates the culture in so many imperceptible ways. Prejudice becomes a sinister problem when we deny that it is out there. You have to admit its existence before you can begin to challenge its presence and effects.

Several teachers disclosed the following perceptions and emotions:

TEACHER: After viewing *The Eye of the Storm,* I began to better understand and accept the fact that specific expectations on the part of the teacher will produce specific behaviors on the part of children. There were many times in the past that I had read about the "self-fulfilling prophecy," but I chose to deny my part in any such phenomenon. You know, it's always easier to identify another teacher as the culprit who exercises such injurious behavior; it's far more difficult to point a finger at yourself. Sitting in a room full of my colleagues and listening to them express guilt and pain for past misdeeds seemed to allow an introspection that I was incapable of before. Finger pointing was not necessary because we were all guilty of the same unchecked behavior.

TEACHER: As an economically disadvantaged, black male who grew up in an inner-city neighborhood, the existence of prejudice is a given. I have no idea as to what life might be without it. I suppose that is why I was so grateful to work with a black, female principal who had comparable childhood experiences. I knew that if Carole was any kind of a leader at all, she would not permit prejudice to continue in her school as part of any "hidden agenda."

At one of those early group meetings, one of the teachers insisted that she had a right to her views, however prejudiced they might be. Carole looked her straight in the eye for what seemed like a real long time. Then she leaned forward in her chair and in this real soft voice said, "Wouldn't it be wonderful if we could get past judging someone by their color, or dialect, or hair texture? Maybe then we could focus on issues of hunger and homelessness and the kinds of psychological pain that compel young children to consider suicide in the middle of a school day." Carole had chosen her words very carefully, but it was the pain in her eyes that conveyed a message you could not miss.

TEACHER: It's kind of hard to describe those early meetings. It was as if everyone's heart and mind were in the same place. Do you know what I mean? Have you ever experienced a moment where every person in the room lets their guard down and puts aside their professional facade? Well, that's what it was like at those meetings. We were all focused on helping each other so we could then help the kids in our classrooms. It was as if our individual egos became one collective ego, and together we had the power to make a difference. I felt such a renewed passion about my work as a teacher. There seemed to be a point to everything, after all.

It was during the course of these early rap sessions and constructive dialogues among Carole and her staff that a new mindset began to emerge. Individuals were no longer going it alone, but were forming substantial alliances. They began to move from monolithic modes of thought, conversation, and interaction to consideration of alternative directions and solutions. Moreover, the "if only" outlook began to diminish as teacher reflection and interaction promoted "if I" and "if we" perspectives.

Joe Garcia recollected the early signs of change during these staff development meetings in this way:

The nature of the initial staff meeting was predictable in just about every way. You could just feel the tension, the anger, the negativity. Each and every person in that room wanted to strike out in frustration, but the question was "At whom do you strike?" Several of the teachers just broke down and cried because they were so emotionally distraught. Many verbalized the feeling that they had lost sight of what their profession was all about or why they had chosen to become teachers in the first place. As a whole, this staff was about as depressed as any group could get under similar circumstances.

Over the course of several meetings, the teachers began to regain their own emotional stability. They were no longer struggling in isolated cubicles called classrooms. They were beginning to reach out to each other in search of support and help. There is no doubt in my mind that the initiative to do so emanated from the strength of a principal who was the first to say, "I don't know how to turn things around all by myself. Please help me." In this way, Carole began to build a coalition, an alliance whose power emerged more from their determination of heart and soul than from their numbers.

It was at this point that they were ready to reinstate their positions as effective, caring *professionals*. I can't overstate the word and the meaning it carried because it was not a distraught or psychologically defeated group of individuals who turned things around. It was a determined team of professionals who made a commitment to work together and help each other in order to regain control and take charge of their school. In some elusive way, change had already begun.

Garman (1982) captured the dynamics that appear to have come into play during the staff development sessions described above:

When a group of educators comes together in an educational alliance there is opportunity for the unit to become involved in a rich encounter with a heightened sense of reciprocity. The term synchronicity is often used to describe this condition. It is when the participants work harmoniously toward achieving their own goals and the goals of the group.... [A]t some point members are able to accept each other's "realness" with a degree of compassion, respect, and eventually with genuine affection. Second, the group begins to function with an optimum level of dynamic tension.

The extreme anxieties due to individual differences have been reduced: the level of dissonance and discord has been dissipated. Yet the individuals in the group remain interesting enough to one another that they offer stimulation and challenge as well as a sense of commitment. Part of the dynamic tension is generated by each individual's own fascinating inner world. They find themselves learning from each other in very different ways. The other aspect of dynamic tension comes from the excitement that spawns a collective spirit as a result of the recognition that the aims and action of the group are toward worthy goals. Members are said to be "in sync" with one another, thereby regenerating the collective spirit and then revitalizing themselves from it as they work together. (p. 48)

BUILDING A COALITION WITHIN THE NETWORK

The network that was forming in and around B. F. Day also needed a forum—what Barbara Endicott called "a clearinghouse for energy and ideas." The Building-Based Management Committee, which was open to staff, parents, and any interested members of the community, was transformed into the Site Council by Lory Misel, a clinical social worker in both the public and the private sector with 30 years of experience. Lory had been an instructor and guest lecturer at several Washington universities and had led programs for school administrators throughout the United States and Canada on such topics as preventing and managing school tragedies, creating a caring school climate, caring and self-esteem training for educators, healing at-risk kids, self-control, and repairing relationships.

At initial meetings in the spring of 1990, Carole explained to Lory that even though KOOL-IS was improving things somewhat, there was still some dissension among the staff, that parents of neighborhood children were extremely angry at the school, and that in general the school in its old building had had a very negative feeling. Lory had two ideas. In order to enhance school life through monetary and in-kind donations, he suggested forming an independent foundation to handle the legal and financial issues. The B. F. Day Foundation is now supervised by the lawyer volunteers who helped set it up. Lory's other idea was to work in a structured way to create the environment that would justify B. F. Day's calling itself "The Family School." To this end, he began to teach the staff a better way to organize their school.

Lory explained that three organizational structures have existed throughout history: military, governmental, and family. Both the governmental and the military structures are inherently inappropriate for schools because they are designed to organize and coordinate massive numbers of adults. In addition, the military structure is based on a "we/they," "good guys/bad guys" mentality, and both the military and the governmental mindsets encourage thinking in terms of "strategic planning," "teams," and "competition." By contrast, the family structure fosters a higher level of functioning so that all members can become responsive, interactive, and flexible. Unfortunately, most schools are organized on a military or governmental model.

Lory taught the B. F. Day participants that the nature of a school's organizational structure becomes obvious in it's "form" (its classroom management, lesson plans, meetings, paperwork—anything that is a daily requirement) and its "content" (the emotional energy that is created and expended in the accomplishment of the form). He has identified two types of content that reflect our own natures: prosocial content and antisocial content. When our content is prosocial, we are kind and cooperative; we have a sense of trust, a sense of belonging, and wish to be of service and help to others. When our content is antisocial, we are angry, distrustful, and competitive; we have a primary wish to get, rather than to give.

If a school is focused solely on accomplishing its form—on getting its tasks done—it will unconsciously create an antisocial climate for the staff, students, and parents. In contrast, by consciously focusing on creating and maintaining a prosocial climate, everyone exceeds even their own expectations. Because neither the governmental nor the military model meets the emotional needs of children, schools should avoid them. The family model can be adapted to fit the school when one remembers that the school "family" is the one extended group that all the children share and in which they all can have similar experiences.

Lory has observed that when a program designed to change the emotional content from antisocial to prosocial is introduced in a school, feelings are intense. Teachers who by nature are not prosocial see the program as a threat because they have a hard time justifying the changes that will occur. For example, if a teacher is used to feeling outraged by a child's outburst and used to putting the child outside the classroom door, how will that teacher deal with the concept that every student is inherently kind and that anger and outbursts should be interpreted as requests for kindness and inclusion? Lory commented:

> Prosocial teachers are really good teachers. They say, "Of course. This [new orientation] is what we need to do." Those teachers who identify with their antisocial nature say things like, "This is pie in the sky. You're going to lose control of the kids. It's not going to work." These same teachers feel that it takes time, that it's not reality, and it is those antisocial teachers who tend not to come to the meetings....

Over the course of several months, first in meetings with the staff and then in the Site Council meetings, Lory taught participants to learn to put this prosocial philosophy to work on a daily basis. Although many of these notions seem familiar, what is novel is that they are being demanded not of the students in this instance, but of the staff and community volunteers:

> We are a family. We join with each other to practice being kind, cooperative, and happy; to learn and to be of service to each other, the school, the community, the world.... We treat people with ...

respect. We keep our word. We keep our home, school, and world
safe, clean, and beautiful. We are kind, helpful, and honest, even
when others do not notice. Our goal is happiness. We accept that
all problems have successful solutions where everybody wins. We
are polite and respectful. We can say and mean "please," "thank
you," "you are welcome," "I appreciate," and "I am sorry" if we forget and act unkindly. We can say what we think, feel, and want. We
are never "bad" people. Sometimes we just forget we are kind, good,
helpful people.

When teachers follow these tenets they are able to tell one another
and their students how important they are and what good things they
have seen them do, as well as that they are needed and loved and appre-
ciated by their family school. Anyone who has worked in a school environment will sense immediately how rare and yet how evocative these
statements are.

According to Lory, Carole's leadership style was the key to making
the change to a prosocial family organizational style at B. F. Day:

Really good schools are principal-dependent. If you have a school
that is really cooking and really doing a great job, you will notice
that it has a charismatic leader. Just out of sheer force of that
principal's personality and professional skills, he or she is able to
change the school effectively....

If you have 20% of the staff that are prosocial and a principal
who is emotionally into it, it creates energy and more people
come on board. It is a process of attitudinal healing. You cannot
change the world, but you can change your mind.

Lory described for me the way the structure of the Site Council
reflects the school's new prosocial orientation:

The Site Council meets once a month. Meetings begin promptly at
6:30 P.M. and end precisely at 8:00 P.M., and each one begins with a
celebration of accomplishments and successes, both personal and
relating to school. Anyone can attend. It is not a discussion group.
It is not permitted to talk about problems, worries, and expectations. You always have people who are plugged into their antisocial
behavior who want to come in and bitch, moan, and complain. At
a Site Council meeting, that is just not permitted.

It is permitted, however, to set up the small committees that work
on problems, to hear reports on accomplishments, and to hear reports

from committees whose work is stuck and who would like some help. The agenda consists of items carried over from the previous meeting, members' requests during the month, and spontaneous suggestions. The people who preside are "Father Goose" and "Mother Goose." This terminology is used because "this is a meeting at an elementary school; this is not a government or military institution." While one "goose" leads, the other takes notes. Within two days of each meeting, a copy of what went on will be in every mailbox in school and distributed to all parents. According to Lory:

> Whenever you get frightened parents, it is because they are lacking information. One way to decrease fear is to give people information. At the Site Council meetings, there are no secrets.
> Whether you attend or not, all parents, staff, and students should have the right to know what's going on.

Lory told me that the goal of the meeting is not necessarily to accomplish business, as we think of business, but rather to practice and enjoy prosocial behavior. Each time that happens, he has observed, the positive energy of the Site Council permeates the school. Gripers are encouraged to take charge of the problem they are complaining about by working in a small committee or to see Mother or Father Goose after the meeting. Those who can enhance their prosocial behaviors tend to get involved in the work; those who cannot tend to stop coming to meetings and impeding progress.

The Site Council also affords a place where highly motivated parents and community members can attract others to work with them on innovative projects. One such parent is Paul Quay, who has two children in the school and lives in the neighborhood. As an early member of the Building-Based Management Committee and then of the Site Council, he felt that the preponderance of high-needs students at B. F. Day and the resulting number of special programs caused disruption that kept average children from receiving appropriate instruction. He was also creatively interested in the answers to these questions:

> What are our teaching goals? How do we increase academic achievement? How do we provide a safe enviroment in which to learn? How do we make B. F. Day a school of choice for parents? How do we graduate students with self-esteem and concern for their community?

Paul, who is an associate professor of oceanography at the University of Washington, actively pursued his goals. He and a teacher wrote proposals that resulted in grants from NASA for the study of weather and from Partners in Public Education for a microscope camera (a camera attachment that transmits whatever is on the microscope slide onto a television screen so that all the children can see it at the same time) and equipment to measure water quality (pH balance, temperature, salt content, algal abundance) in rain, streams, and lakes. He told me:

> The focus of the Site Council over the last couple of years has evolved from defining our school goals to implementing change. Progress is slow, but at least we have a forum to ask questions that are on the minds of the staff, parents, and community and develop plans to answer them....
>
> The involvement my wife and I have had at B. F. Day for the last five years gives us some insight into the ingredients necessary to succeed with the diverse population at [the school]. The principal has to have vision and management skills. The teaching staff has to be committed. The parents must be involved. Volunteers play a vital role. Interaction with the neighborhood community is enriching. Hopefully, B. F. Day will become the school of choice for more and more parents. If this occurs, it will be a strong indicator of our success.

It is clear that B. F. Day has already become the school of choice for those who have experienced its prosocial atmosphere. When Lory suggested that the school should have its own song because music binds people together, Jo Daly, the music teacher, obliged with an image of the ideal set to bouncy music that is now on the lips of every child and adult in the building:

> Oh, what do they say about B. F. Day?
> They say it's the family school
> Where sharing and caring, and lending a hand
> We all form a family
> Across the land
>
> Oh, what do they say about B. F. Day?
> Come visit, and you will see
> All our smiles go for miles
> You're a friend to the end
> At B. F. Day!

CHAPTER 8

Breaking the Bureaucratic Mold: A "Family School" in Action

In attempting to uncover the concrete organizational features of this program, such as specific project designs, job guidelines, and outlines of participant responsibilities that might prove useful in the understanding and replication of this model at other school sites, I uncovered the basic way the mindset of "family schools" applies to the behavior of staff. Carole proclaimed:

> Educators are accustomed to abiding by a regimen of systematized, uniformed, and scheduled activities and interactions. It was this school's collective dissatisfaction with those very ineffectual ideologies that spawned the KOOL-IS program.

On any given day, a teacher may assume the role of a community volunteer as she drives a mother and child to a nearby clinic after school or as she assists in arranging for furniture pickup and delivery with acquaintances at a local church. A community volunteer may assume the role of teacher when she accompanies three children on an outing to a supermarket and explains the value of reading a nutrition label on the side of a cereal box. A case manager may assume the temporary role of school secretary so that the secretary may walk a new student and parent through the school halls and introduce them to people on staff. "There is no precise order to the way activities are carried out or any rhyme or reason as to why one person may conduct an interaction as opposed to another," according to Carole.

The ideology that underlies the success of this project is that all people have something to offer and are most effectual when allowed to diversify their roles in order to attain personal fulfillment while at the same time meeting the needs of others. But still, how does one orga-

Janet Jones Preston, family support worker: "If 'it is not my job,' tell me, whose job is it?" (Photo: Jim Bates/*Education Week*)

nize interactions in such a way that this ideology works to everyone's advantage? Apparently, the same way one organizes the interactions and activities in any family—through personal and often spontaneous communication. Carole proposed this analogy:

> Suppose that dad is a better cook than mom. Is it okay for dad to step outside his role as sole breadwinner and put on an apron? As long as he's not stepping on mom's toes, why shouldn't he? For that matter, mom might want to try her hand at fixing the car, even though the activity doesn't fit her traditional role as housekeeper. And if junior decides to do the laundry before running bases with mom, all the better.
>
> If another school wishes to replicate what we are doing at B. F. Day, the principal and staff will have to restructure their thought processes regarding the school as an institution of education. We think of our school as a family, and just like any other family, there are good days and bad days, ups and downs, conflicts and disagreements, celebrations and victories.
>
> Dad is not the sole breadwinner. Mom is not the old-fashioned housewife of yesteryear. Families no longer run according to a rigid role assignment; neither can schools if they are to become humane, caring, and nurturing places where everyone has a sense of belonging and being needed.

Obviating or circumventing old maxims, precepts, and traditional dictates allows a school to transmit psychological and social services spontaneously and effectively. The form, flow, and timing of these services can be adjusted and fine-tuned based on the immediate needs of recipients. Moreover, the cohesion of small, committed teams of teachers, one family support worker, one case manager, and a dozen volunteers ensures the continuity and reliability of services on which trust is founded.

Seen in this way, the KOOL-IS program might best be described as the translation of values, beliefs, and principles of an entire school into an operational frame of mind, or set of ideological criteria on which many, many strategic decisions will be based. This platform of implicit standards represents the purpose or rallying point from which people can connect in aspiring toward a common cause. Nontraditional ways of operating and behaving set the tone and climate of the school and seem to communicate the principles to which participants in this school give allegiance. It is this set of principles, beliefs, and values that reflects the cultural ethos and integrity of B. F. Day.

A perfect example of this is observable in the extraordinary attitude of de facto faculty member Diann Mize. She is the crackerjack school secretary who demonstrates many talents while she juggles administrative and therapeutic roles with teachers, parents, and students. As the first person met by any parent or child enrolling in the school, she consciously sets the tone of a warm and welcoming environment. Her reasoning is clear:

> "Homeless" is a title that any of us could wear at any time. I try
> to face each day working with the staff, the children, and their
> families in such a way that if I were on the receiving end, I would
> feel worthwhile. I see so many people who have so little and are
> referred to as "them." They are not "them." They are "us"
> because at any time, we could be in their place.

SUBJECTIVE REALITIES OF CHANGE

Viewing the changes that occurred at B. F. Day from the perspective of individual and collective meaning, one can see that a sense of anxiety, imposition, ambivalence, and resistance all played a part. Any successful attempt to reconstruct a philosophy of schooling in another school—any other school—will require a more substantial understanding both of what change entails and of the role each of us plays as an individual within a cohesive group.

It has often been stated that the single most important idea in this regard is that change is a process, not an event (Fullan & Park, 1981; G. Hall & Loucks, 1977). "Real change, whether desired or not, represents a serious personal and collective experience characterized by ambivalence and uncertainty" (Fullan, 1991, p. 32). The essence of any change is rarely clear at the outset. During the period of transition, as individuals attempt to assimilate more information than perhaps they can handle the "tenacity of conservatism" will prevail as a natural and inevitable phenomenon (Marris, 1975, p. 2).

According to Fullan (1991), numerous factors affect the process of educational change, among them: subjective realities of ambivalence and uncertainty about the status quo and pressure to maintain it; the reality-based or "contrived" need for change reflected in a problem-solving orientation versus an opportunistic (bureaucratic) orientation; generative leadership or apathy on the part of the school principal; power sharing among principal, teachers, and parents; a collegial environment that fosters a sense of problem ownership versus a sense of isolationism in which teachers are left to sink or swim alone; the relationship between teacher and child; and parent involvement.

To understand how major accomplishments are achieved, it is necessary to understand both the content and the subjective realities of any change action (Barth, 1990; Schlechty, 1990). To overlook the subjective realities of the change process is to court the unsuccessful outcome of an innovation. For more than "surface change" to occur, individuals must understand and share the underlying principles and rationale on which the practical change is founded (Little, 1982; Rutter, Maugham, Mortimer, Ouston, & Smith, 1979; Yee, 1987).

MORE THAN THE JOB DESCRIPTION: THE FAMILY SUPPORT WORKER

Evidence of the profoundness of the change in mindset that has permitted the staff at B. F. Day to function as a role-shifting family can also be found in the "above-and-beyond-the-call" behavior of Janet Jones Preston. Her designation as family support worker at B. F. Day came about as part of a social service, school-based demonstration project conceived in 1988 and jointly funded and initiated by the city of Seattle and the United Way. Janet, an African-American woman in her late thirties, holds a baccalaureate degree in English literature and minority studies and has been a paraprofessional in special education in the Seattle elementary, middle, and high schools.

I was never formally introduced to Janet, but rather discovered her unpacking some boxes in an unusual school-based office that can only be described as having the ambience of a small country store. Sweaters, pants, shirts, and an assortment of scarves and gloves were neatly arranged on tables. There were different-sized shoes stacked on what may once have functioned as gym bleachers. Dresses and coats hung from two racks strategically positioned between an oak filing cabinet and a wall mirror. An open cabinet drawer revealed a stash of children's socks, underpants, and undershirts.

Corrugated boxes offered an array of toys and games. A pitcher of orange juice and a plate of cookies sat next to drawing paper, crayons, and scissors. This crowded little room exuded a warmth and cozyness that left one no choice but to feel right at home.

From behind an open closet door, an extremely pretty face popped out and requested my assistance with some heavy boxes filled with canned food. I gave it and proceeded to have a comfortable conversation with this young, petite black woman despite the fact that I had yet to introduce myself. But introductions were not necessary because Janet knows no strangers. She is real, unpretentious, and does not know the meaning of the word *can't*. A job outline has not yet been written to describe the way this family support worker does her job. Janet expressed her feelings in this way:

> Youngsters come in here every day. They are hungry, they are tired, they are poorly dressed. Many are worried about where they will sleep on any given night. Their eyes are like mirrors into their little souls—sad and empty. They have no sense of belonging and no sense of hope. Most of them are frightened and feel very much alone.
>
> They don't need to be tested, evaluated, or scrutinized. They need to be loved, cared for, nurtured, and made to feel that they belong someplace.
>
> These children do not need professional people in their lives. They need warm, caring adults who will stand by them and find ways to help them no matter what it takes to do so. They need significant adults who are just as accessible during evening hours and on weekends as they are during school hours.
>
> If an individual is truly committed to helping these kids, no matter what it takes, he will go above and beyond the call of duty outlined in his job description.

DEFINITELY NOT THE OLD BUREAUCRACY: THE ART OF BARTER-STYLE RESOURCE EXCHANGE

An excellent example of the way this changed mindset can break the bureaucratic mold occurred when the supply of affordable housing looked rather bleak. Janet came across an article in the *Seattle Times* that relayed the details of "a building allegedly taken over by neighborhood gang members and drug dealers, resulting in possible court action to shut down and board up the premises." Vigilant for any opportunity, Janet wasted no time in attaining much-needed apartments for school families. The story is illustrative in that she avoided bureaucratic channels and went right to the source—the landlord.

One of the attorneys affiliated with the case, Raymond Connell, recollected the situation:

> By the winter of 1990, the Garfield Apartments had allegedly been taken over by neighborhood gang members and drug deal-

ers. As a result, the physical conditions and social climate of the premises began to deteriorate at a rapid pace.

The landlord, Mr. Mitchell, had no choice but to evict those tenants directly involved in the use and/or dealing of abusive substances. In doing so, the majority of apartments [became] vacant. The problem then became one of finding new tenants so that vagrants would not begin to vandalize the property and occupy hallways and stairwells.

Janet continued the story:

> I found myself thinking about the odd way in which the system perpetuates homelessness. It seemed strange that we could have so many empty apartments without people and at the same time have so many people without apartments.... Here was a situation where I had the people and this landlord had the living space. It was an opportunity not to be lost. I approached Raymond Connell in front of the church we both attend. He was most receptive to my ideas and agreed to give me his client's phone number....
>
> I called Mr. Mitchell, introduced myself, and opened the conversation by stating that I thought I could help him and I knew he could help me. Mr. Mitchell listened and seemed pensive for a number of minutes. I just had to get him to agree, and so I kept talking until he could see that this was a mutually advantageous opportunity. That phone conversation was a major turning point.

Sarason (1977) proclaims that individuals as well as agencies have to "figure out possible ways in which [they] can learn to exchange resources in mutually beneficial ways and without finances being a prerequisite for discussion or the basis for exchange." He suggests that we ask, "What do I have that somebody else can use in exchange for something of his that I need?" In the case of the Garfield Apartments, Janet could provide the tenantry that would be most useful to Mr. Mitchell, who had the vacant apartments at risk of vandalism or court closure. By simply redefining existing resources for housing homeless families, Janet significantly diminished the disparity between the needs of her clients and the limited ability of the community to meet those needs by providing affordable housing.

Moreover, Janet reached outside her tightly knit network of collaborative coworkers when she approached attorney Connell at their church. By doing so, she extended her network; and through the dyadic links of one family support worker and one landlord, a self-transforming network came about as one individual connected to the next and the next. Within a short span of time, homeless families were placed in the Garfield Apartments and permanent housing became a reality for many. First-month rent deposits for all new tenants were drawn from the KOOL-IS access fund under the direction of Atlantic Street Center case managers. Mr. Mitchell proceeded to hire Gary and Claire, a homeless couple, to act as building managers.

A NEW BREED OF BUILDING MANAGERS

During an informal visit I had with Gary and his wife Claire, I gained further insights as they talked about their perception of building management. Both fair-haired, blue-eyed, tall, and thin, this married couple looked like sister and brother. There was something in their mannerisms, in their soft-spoken style, that seemed naive; yet they proved to be most insightful and wise.

The financial burdens of putting two sons through college, compounded by a series of unexpected emotional and medical crises, had left this couple facing middle age without employment and without a home. In spite of this, they perceived themselves as "quite fortunate in the way [they were] able to cope with life's hard knocks and help others to do the same."

Claire, looking somewhat older than her 40 years, excused the shabbiness of their apartment as she served coffee on a makeshift table— a large crate found behind a nearby supermarket. She suggested that I not lean back on the wall "because of the roach situation." She sat on a wobbly wooden chair near a cracked open window and spoke almost in a whisper:

> I'm tired. I'm so tired that sometimes I just want to give up. It isn't easy being homeless. It takes the soul right out of you. But I'm a super now, and I'm proud of that. This apartment may not look like much. I mean the whole building needs to be renovated, but it beats living in a station wagon for five months.
>
> Years ago, the old-time supers knew everyone in their building on a first-name basis. If the super spotted some kids misbehaving or moving in the direction of trouble, he let their parents know. There was a caring relationship between people living in that building.
>
> Today, it's no longer that way. Gary and I don't have a great deal of education, but we know the value of reaching out to other people. In our building, we try to be more like the old-time supers.

There have been countless nights when I have had children knock at our door because their mother didn't return home after dark. Those kids need to have a caring adult reassure them that their mom will eventually return. I keep the kids with us until she does. I give them chocolate chip cookies and milk and let them sleep on our couch.

Some of these families have lived in shelters for so long that they have forgotten how to make a real home. I take the time to show these moms how to cook an inexpensive meal. They are so used to ordering in a pizza or buying several Big Macs that they don't realize the same $8 can fill the refrigerator with fresh fruit and homemade tuna salad and cold cuts.

Being a building manager means more than changing light bulbs in stairwells and collecting the rent. We kind of see ourselves as "connected" to our tenants. They're our neighbors, so we help them. Gary and I have been here for almost a year now, thanks to Mr. Mitchell.

If the school had still perceived itself as shackled to the bureaucracy, the apartment house would have gone empty, many children would not have had a caring adult to reassure them in the night, and two homeless, unemployed, but capable individuals would have had neither home nor jobs. By attending to realities that cried out for new solutions—solutions well beyond any stipulated in an official job description—the family support worker embraced the process of change and turned it into the process of achievement.

CHAPTER 9

"I Am Not a Case Number!
I Am a Mother with Children!"

Parents of children attending B. F. Day were willing to help me come to understand KOOL-IS by telling me where they had been, where they were going, and where they hoped they would never have to go. In describing their lives, they depicted an arduous and sometimes grueling day-to-day existence.

Picking through piles of used and tattered clothing amidst a throng of unkempt shoppers at a Salvation Army store or the local Goodwill was described as an exercise in futility. Finding a laundromat offering coin-operated washers and dryers that required only three quarters per load as opposed to six might involve walking two to four miles. Food shopping seemed more like a wearisome process than a single event, for without a car the task of carrying several packages back to the transitional shelter called "home" often involved two or three trips to the same place. Fare for public transportation was conserved for longer trips across town to obtain food stamps, medical health assistance, and gas and electric utility coupons, as well as to make required weekly visits to social workers. Fragmentation of social services often translated into four to six bus rides in the course of one day.

Overcoming the hurdles of long distances, time, bad weather conditions, and crying babies fussing on shoulder or hip, the physically and emotionally depleted mother then had to tolerate the impersonalization of a bureaucratic system she did not understand but to which she had to acquiesce.

Lena, a 30-year-old, single parent of two boys, aged 7 and 2, described the way in which she experienced the bureaucratic division of social services:

Ronda White and her children: "I just know that the school knew who I was, and they cared about me, and they wouldn't let my kids wind up on the streets." (Photo: Barry Wong/*Seattle Times*)

Why, it just ain' worth the trip. You wait for hours to see your social worker for five whole minutes. Sometimes she ain' there and you be talkin' to another face. That face maybe don' even know your name and maybe she talk fast and mean cause she out of patience. You be tryin' to get somewhere even the littlest bit, and you have to deal with some uppity attitude sittin' behind a big desk. I tell you, you gotta psych yourself for that trip. It don' make no sense.

Anyway, whoever it is, she ask the same questions every time and write down the same answers on the same form. I know that form cause it's the blue color one. You see the yellow one they use at the medical clinic where you get the prescription for the child's medicines. And the orange form, well that's for the utility coupons so you have light. 'Cause they shut those lights off if you don' get your name on an orange form. You be sittin' in the cold and the dark with a sick baby in your arms if you ever skip the trip for the orange form. Anyway, she write down some things, and then she give you $2 so's you can get yourself on another bus and go to another place where you wait your turn again, and then you watch whiles the person fill out a differen' color paper.

Each form supposed to take away one small piece of my problems. That's what I been told. But you know what I think? There ain' no color form that can take away the pain and sadness from a human being. 'Cause you talkin' about a whole person, and that person don' suffer one piece of their problems or their pain at a time. You not goin' to get your kids out of poverty no how, no matter what color the form is and no matter how long the bus ride you take. That's the only thing I knowd for sure.

Lena's sense of psychological defeat became apparent as she spoke, and she is not alone. Other mothers recounted similar experiences.

Barbara, youthful and attractive in appearance, is raising her 6-year-old granddaughter, Shari, alone. Concerned about "Shari's well-being in a home where people were going nowhere and were content to stagnate in their own misery," Barbara made the difficult decision to leave Florida with her grandchild and start over again with the help of a cousin in Seattle.

I came to Seattle feeling secure that I could reside with my cousin and her family, at least for a brief time. After two weeks, the landlord insisted that I leave on a day's notice. I couldn't jeopardize my cousin's well-being, so I found myself on the street with a 5-year-old and no place to go. The details of my story are not as important as the fact that I did find a place to live in spite of "the system."...

Every time I attempted to take advantage of the so-called services available to me, I found myself walking into one obstacle after another. You aren't eligible for this unless you have that. But you can't get that because you filled out the wrong form at the wrong time for the wrong thing. I'd often say to myself, "Barbara, if you want to get anywhere, you are going to have to get a college degree just so you can understand all the requirements and rules that seem to make so much sense to everyone but you."

Lisbeth Schorr (1988) confirmed the hidden obstacles within a large-scale, bureaucratic social service system as she considered the perspective of the client:

Families with few supports but great needs are often inept at using available supports, formal or informal. They often need help in using help. They are unlikely to be able to make good use of services offered in circumstances that may meet professional and bureaucratic requirements but do not sufficiently take into account the obstacles faced by very depleted families. (p. 155)

Barbara recounted her initial experience with the staff at B. F. Day and expressed her tremendous relief in discovering the support they offered:

The very first time I walked through the doors of this school, I knew something was different—I mean different. People actually smiled at you and asked if they could be of assistance. I was definitely not prepared for this environment. At first, I was somewhat mistrusting. It isn't everyday that people are pleasant and treat you with a bit of respect....

Anyway, on that first day, I met Carole Williams and Janet and a whole bunch of wonderful people. Mrs. Williams said, "This is a family school. That means we are here to help both you and your granddaughter. Please let us know the ways in which we can best help you." I wasn't sure if I had lost my hearing or my mind!... I have never heard of a school caring about a parent. Okay, if you are lucky you come across a teacher that will take your child under her wing during the school day. But this was something else. I felt so relieved by the end of that first day at the school because I thought, "Finally, someone is there to help me get help."

CASE MANAGEMENT

Assignment of an on-site primary case manager to a family that appears to be immobilized by an overwhelming array of unmet needs has proven to have the most potential for communicating and substantiating the message that a parent is not alone in carrying out child-rearing responsibilities. As a distinctive component of the KOOL-IS model, one or two case managers are assigned to work at the school site itself.

In the initial stages of the program, Robert Mann was the B. F. Day case manager. As the program expanded to other schools in the district, Robert became the director of the case management program and began to work out of an office based at the Atlantic Street Center. His role at B. F. Day was assumed by Simeon Fields, currently the only case manager working at the school site. Simeon has worked with up to 10 families at any one time.

Simeon and all other case managers who have been assigned to schools in the district report directly to Robert Mann for supervision of all cases. Should the caseload become too great, or should the on-site case manager find himself or herself working with a particularly difficult family, the course of action is determined by staff at the Atlantic Street Center, who are extremely well qualified in the area of social services.

The Atlantic Street Center assumes responsibility for training primary case managers, with or without a college degree, "who appear to have a natural inclination for working with people in distress." According to Robert Mann:

> We often get hung up with educational status when in reality there are a great many individuals out there who have a natural instinct for working with overwhelmed moms and their kids. Sometimes, a less educated but more streetwise case manager-in-training can show greater insight and greater empathy for the downtrodden than an experienced veteran in the field of social work or human relations.
>
> Individuals who have "been there," so to speak, have the advantage of an insider's perspective. When you have been treated badly during the course of your own life experience, you don't forget what it feels like, and you don't need a textbook in psychology to explain it. So if you're asking whether our case managers are Harvard grads, the answer is "no." But not all Harvard grads could deal with an angry, hostile, or suicidal homeless person.
>
> Our training of case managers does not require a great deal

of reading, writing, and research. It has more to do with developing a vigilance and sensitivity to what's actually happening out there on the street. Rather than being well read in the sociological literature, a good case manager has to be "in sync" with a client in distress.

The nature and function of the primary case manager evolves and is redefined in direct response to the gradually disclosed, unique, and often unarticulated needs of the individual family. The case manager sustains a supportive contact with student and family throughout the delivery of multiple services rendered by diverse social service and community agencies.

Assuming the role of a "broker," the case manager does more than merely make referrals; he or she provides prereferral counseling for those families who are unreceptive to or mistrusting of outside social service agencies, and personally accompanies the student and family members to the referral agency. In further assuming the role of "family advocate," the case manager enacts a third-party role to facilitate communications with disparate service agencies and the many different bureaucracies rendering help of one kind or another.

Lenora Rubin, a mental health consultant with the Seattle school district, concisely described the crucial role of intervention personnel:

> When you work with families in crisis, it is crucial to have caring personnel who are trained or have a natural way in working with those who may be ornery, or disrespectful, or just plain hurting. In light of their misfortunate histories, many impoverished adults and youngsters have little expectation of others as reliable, trustworthy, helpful, or truly committed to making a difference on a one-on-one basis.
>
> Often, it is not the goals or strategies of a particular program that lead to successful outcomes; rather, it is the elusive qualities that constitute caring and trusting bonds between people whose life experiences are quite different.

In describing the essence of those programs that have proven most successful with a large number of multiproblem families, Lisbeth Schorr (1988) captured the features of case management as it is employed at B. F. Day:

> In these programs someone takes responsibility for assuring that child and family needs are in fact met, regardless of bureaucratic

or professional compartments. No one says, "this may be what you need, but helping you get it is not part of my job or outside our jurisdiction."...

Professionals venture outside their own familiar surroundings to provide services in nontraditional settings, including homes, and often at nontraditional hours.... Successful programs try to reduce the barriers—of money, time, fragmentation, geographic, and psychological remoteness—that make heavy demands on those with limited energy and organizational skills. (pp. 258–259)

FOSTERING MUTUAL OBLIGATION
BETWEEN SCHOOL AND PARENT

The promise of a lifeline engenders a collaboration between parent and school that might not otherwise develop. The very nature of the services provided by the school, and the terms on which services are offered, legitimize the parent's sense of worthiness. As their unarticulated psychological needs are met, parents gradually develop a sense of being valued not only for who they are but for who they can be. A network of communication and "mutual obligation" facilitates the parent's role as a partner in the successful accomplishments of the school.

The case story of Ronda, a single parent of four children, all of them under the age of 9, captures the essence of collaboration between parent and school and the way in which the school fosters conditions of mutual obligation.

> I wasn't homeless in Houston, but I felt I had to leave for my children's well-being. I came to Seattle because someone told me it was the place for a woman with little kids. As soon as I got into the bus station, I started calling places trying to get somewhere to stay. We stayed in the YWCA shelter for almost a month before we went into the Seattle emergency housing shelter, and we stayed there almost two months.
>
> It's like you're moving from place to place and the kids can't settle themselves. Their minds are not working right, their brains are not working right, they're just not stable at all. Then, sometime or other, I enrolled them at B. F. Day.
>
> That family support worker, Janet, I took to her right away. She said, "Ronda, if it's this you need, or that you need, or whatever you need, all you have to do is call on us and we will help you." I was stunned, you know, because like at other schools they

don't know you and you don't know them.

So if I didn't have the money for the kids' notebooks and school supplies and the kids didn't have no decent clothes or shoes, the people at the school just helped me right away. If it wasn't for the KOOL-IS program, I wouldn't have an apartment.

I tried to get the deposit from my social worker, you know. But they don't bend no rules at the agency, and so by the time they do all the paperwork with the forms and this and that, well the landlord ain't exactly waitin' on you with the apartment. He's gonna rent it to the first person that have the cash. So I called Mrs. Preston, and she told me to talk to Robert Mann. She said, "He will help you out. So don't fret about the rent, the light bill, or what have you."

So I called Mr. Mann, and he said not to worry. He asked me for my landlord's name and address and told me that he would contact him and forward the rent money. If it wasn't for Robert Mann and Janet Preston—there was nobody else that I could turn to for help.

You see, you have to have the bus fare to get to the agencies that can help you. And then you have to take the babies with you and wait for hours so they could fill out these forms and then maybe the agency can help you and then maybe they won't. You have to qualify, like you have to be homeless for a certain number of days or weeks. I don't understand how it all works. I just know that maybe the social service agency would give me the rent money and maybe they wouldn't. And I just know that the school knew who I was, and they cared about me, and they wouldn't let my kids wind up on the streets.

After I got my apartment, some nice volunteers helped me get furniture, pots, pans, dishes, bath towels, and bed linen. Most of it was new, and some of it was used but almost like new. Mrs. Preston even got me a broom, a mop and pail, and detergent. I felt so encouraged.

I can't tell you how encouraged I felt. Right away, I got myself a job at Kmart so I could pay the second month's rent. The people at the school was so proud of me. They gave me so much praise— like they knew I was trying to get my act together. I just felt so good about myself. It was just like I was a regular person.

After a few months, I fell and injured my back. I felt real bad, and I began to go back to my old ways. You know, some days I would be so tired, and I would just oversleep, and I would call Mrs. Preston and tell her the kids missed the school bus again.

Mrs. Preston would assure me that she would come get the kids so they wouldn't miss school, and she did. She didn't give me a lecture about oversleeping or not being a responsible parent. She would just say, "I know you will get it together again, Ronda. I believe in you." Nobody ever said that to me before.

In an article titled "[Ap]parent Involvement: Reflections on Parents, Power and Urban Public Schools," Michelle Fine (1993) focused on issues of "parent empowerment." Based on informal interviews with 12 women, Fine stated:

> Many women explained that their personal illnesses could provoke dramatic, adverse consequences for their children's schooling, particularly in terms of attendance and grades. These women sit not only at the nexus of racist, classist, and sexist institutions and violent streets, but they know that when their own resources (e.g., health) go, there is no ease. When their fragile balancing act falls apart, everyone blames them. As is obvious from their narratives, low income mothers are holding together the pieces of a society torn apart by a Federal government that, over the past decade, has shown disdain for, and has severely punished those living in poverty. They themselves are the only thing that holds their lives together. (p. 688)

In attempting to act more like a family than an institution, B. F. Day provides the emotional support many mothers need in order to get their act together, as indicated in the collective resolution of Ronda's dilemma:

> Then one day, Mrs. Preston invited me to have lunch with her at the school. She asked if she could share her dilemma with me and maybe then I could help her. She told me how many children missed the bus each day and how hard it was for her to drive all over town to pick them up. Well, I thought, "What could I do?" Then, Mrs. Preston said that if she could count on me to get my kids off to school, then that would be one thing off her mind.
> I started to think about how much she did for me. The least I could do was help to get my kids on that old school bus so Mrs. Preston wouldn't be rushing over to my place every day. What I'm trying to say is that if I was responsible for my kids, then I would be helping Mrs. Preston because she would have more time to take care of some other mother's child who wasn't being responsible. I made up my mind right then and there that I was gonna get my kids to school on time and you know what? My kids are on that bus every day.

I am a responsible parent. Some days I help the school because I ride the bus as a monitor. Some days I work in the lunchroom or the yard. I help any way that I can.

I used to think that nobody in this world cared about me. If they didn't have this attitude, you know, like we're all part of a big family at the school, I'd be stuck not knowin' who to turn to or where to go. This school care about you. They make you feel like you have something to offer, even though you are poor. There's like a special attitude that the teachers have here. They care about you and your kin, and they don't look down on you because you are different from them in so many ways. They let you have self-respect. Without it, you ain't nobody.

Because the school remains committed and responsive to a family's immediate needs, a sense of trust in the continuity and reliability of those acting as service providers begins to emerge. It is at this point that volunteers may offer more than practical help and venture toward building domains of self-esteem that enable a mother to assume responsibility for her own life and the lives of her children.

A PLACE CALLED "HEAVEN"

Another family's turning point, which I had the opportunity to witness, showed me the helping network's effectiveness in turning squalor into the beginning of a new future.

Debbie, a single parent in her late twenties caring for two boys aged about 9 and 14, had received assistance from KOOL-IS in finding a permanent residence in an efficiency motel room. She earned part of the monthly rent by "working the phones, collecting rent payments for the manager, showing vacant motel rooms to other families, and scrubbing kitchens and baths after people move out." Her sole material possessions consisted of several worn blankets, a suitcase of clothes for the boys and herself, and a teddy bear that Debbie and the boys took turns sleeping with "when someone is real scared." Simeon, B. F. Day's case manager, had drawn up an itemized list of needed furnishings, linens, dishes, flatware, detergents, and grooming products during a visit to Debbie's new home, and he and Janet had contacted members of the Mercer Island United Methodist Church on Debbie's behalf.

On a chilly weekday morning, I accompanied Simeon to meet Debbie and better understand the ways in which the school planned to assist her. We were greeted with a wave and a holler from Debbie's door:

"I'm so glad you could come over. I love having company since I moved into my own place." Auburn hair, hazel eyes, and a bright smile overshadowed Debbie's tattered blouse and pants. She asked us to excuse her bare feet, as her oldest son had borrowed her last pair of socks for gym class. She waved us into her apartment with obvious delight.

We could see the backup of sewage from the toilet into both kitchen sink and bathtub, open and empty cupboards lined with roach traps, and blankets spread on the floor in an otherwise empty room. Still, there was that echo of victory that resounded in Debbie's laughter as she expressed her sense of joy and hopefulness:

> I ask you, is this place Heaven or what? No mice, no rats, no crazies. Best of all, no more shelters. I finally have a home, a private space that belongs to me. When I look around I just fill up with joy 'cause I finally have my own little place.

Four days later, I returned to Debbie's home in Simeon's company. I watched in awe as three community members—a retired attorney, a grandmother, and a pastor—worked a miracle. The attorney, Leo, opened up his box of tools and dismantled water pipes under the sink and toilet. Simeon and Pastor Olive unloaded a small van and reappeared with two twin beds, a sleeper couch, a kitchen table and chairs, linens, dishes, and other essentials—donations from four local families. The energetic and exuberant grandmother, Bev Parker, unloaded her car and carried in one crate of canned foods and another of fresh apples, pears, and oranges donated by a retired teacher.

Bev placed a flowering plant on the kitchen table and told Debbie, "This plant will blossom, as will your family." Debbie started to cry. The pastor said, "Let us hold hands and bless Debbie's new home." Debbie looked straight at me and asked a question for which her tearful eyes revealed the answer: "Is this place Heaven or what?"

PERSONALIZED, COMPREHENSIVE, AND CONTINUOUS SUPPORT

This small-scale, neighborhood school project lacks the grand scheme of a city, state, or national program but appeared to solve the problem of the moment for Debbie and her family with a degree of expedience and with the human elements that the bureaucratic system is ill equipped to provide—compassion, friendship, and ongoing, one-to-one support. Debbie and her children would continue to receive the understanding, nurturance, and care of these and other volunteers who share in a vision of what can be achieved when people put their minds together, roll up their sleeves, and work as a team to break through social barriers and economic inequalities.

More than likely, Debbie would require further assistance, as in the task of obtaining food stamps. A school volunteer, perhaps Bev, would drive Debbie to the appropriate social service agency and "walk her through the steps" of filling out appropriate forms and speaking to the appropriate personnel. Once Debbie got her food stamps, this same, caring volunteer would make timely visits to Debbie's home to teach her how to budget her money, select good foods, and prepare healthy meals.

Unencumbered by the pressure of the typical social worker's tightly structured schedule, the volunteer may also take the time to teach this mother how to organize and accomplish daily household tasks. Rather than tell a mother the value of a clean house, one or more volunteers may pitch in and work at her side as she learns how best to disinfect a bathroom or discovers the most expedient way to launder, fold, arrange, and store clothing, towels, and bed linen within limited drawer or closet space. The children may be assigned specific chores with the understanding, as Bev said, that "a family works best when it works together."

Recognizing that both children and parents are equally important targets of any intervention plan on the part of the school, continuing support services are oriented toward heightening the parents' and children's self-esteem by strengthening their capacity to function effectively on their own behalf.

CHAPTER 10

Enlisting Parents as Partners in Education

At B. F. Day, parents have the opportunity to become well acquainted with their children's teachers. Given the chance to participate actively in parent discussion groups, PTA projects, and professional/lay symposiums, they may become partners in their children's education as they learn, perhaps for the first time, the value of school. The family support worker or an assigned community volunteer will drive them to the school and home again so that they need not face the hurdles of weather, distance, directions, and the cost of public transportation, all of which often impede active parent participation.

Educators, psychologists, and sociologists are in agreement that, as Schorr (1988) has said:

> parents must be made partners with early childhood educators and child development professionals at the local level in new efforts to prepare their children to achieve academic success and social competence. This is especially important for parents who are not well educated and not sophisticated in dealing with large or unfamiliar institutions, and who see themselves as powerless and overwhelmed." (p. 213)

Parents do not receive a lecture on the importance of regular attendance and prompt morning arrivals. Nor do they receive a wake-up call at 7:00 sharp each morning. Rather, they are asked to act as volunteers overseeing a smooth bus ride to and from school several days a week. They may request a position whose minimum wage is donated by local businesses, or they may be among the five or so volunteers each semester in the school library, lunchroom, transition room, or playground. The school family support worker places each parent according to his or her abilities and schedule.

94

Diann Mize, school secretary: "'Homeless' is a title that any of us could wear at any time."

FAMILIARITY BREEDS RESPECT

The most salient feature of the parent volunteer program seems to be the increased opportunity for teachers and mothers to become better acquainted. As one teacher stated, "When two people work together, there is always the chance that a friendship may form. What better friend to have than the parent of a student?"

Numerous studies suggest that the degree of positive interaction between parent and school has a direct impact on the academic performance of students, particularly at-risk students (Dauber & Epstein, 1993; Mortimore et al., 1988; Rosenholtz, 1989; Ziegler, 1987). Rosenholtz (1989) identified differences in parent/teacher relationships based on the social climate of the school. In effective school environments, described as "moving," teachers "focused their efforts on involving parents with academic content, thereby bridging the learning chasm between home and school" (p. 152). To this extent, parents were perceived as part of the solution for improving school life. Conversely, teachers in "stuck" schools "held no goals for parent participation" and in this way projected a limited sense of worth in the role parents might assume in the betterment of student and school life (p. 152).

In considering key factors that differentiated effective from less effective schools, Mortimore and colleagues (1988) stated:

> Our findings show parent involvement in the life of the school to be a positive influence upon pupils' progress and development. This included help in classrooms and on educational visits, and attendance at meetings to discuss children's progress. The headteacher's accessibility to parents was also important; schools operating an informal, pen-door policy being more effective. (p. 255)

To this extent, a parent can become a knowledgeable partner in a child's education with the right encouragement from the school. Dauber and Epstein's (1993) study of parents' attitudes and practices further revealed that:

> Parents' level of involvement is directly linked to the specific practices of the school that encourage involvement at school and guide parents in how to help at home. The data are clear that the school's practices to inform and to involve parents are more important than parent education, family size, marital status, and even grade level in determining whether inner-city parents stay involved with their children's education through the middle grades. (p. 68)

As for the students' perspective, Wilson and Corcoran (1988) concluded:

Participation in school activities by adults other than school staff communicates an important message to students. If adults are willing to take time from their schedules to help schools, it must be an activity of some significance. (p. 117)

From the outset, B. F. Day clearly attempted to build on the power of the parent/school/community connection in an attempt to break the link between poverty and academic failure.

OTHER MOTHERS AS ROLE MODELS

Mothers also find support in talking with other mothers who understand the daily fight for survival because they, too, are economically impoverished. On one rainy and dismal morning, Hanna, a paid lunchroom monitor, Gabrielle, a volunteer tutor during library hour, and Estelle, another parent, shared stories and coping strategies as they snacked on fresh fruit and coffee. Hanna, the 23-year-old single parent of four, explained why she sought to be a partner in the educational experience of her children:

I was 14 when I birthed my first child. That was the end of school for me. It was no big deal 'cause the school buildin' was just a place to hang out anyway. I never really learn' nothin' over there.

My mother, she hated the teachers. She say they was white uppity, you know, like they was better than us. If like the teacher sent home a note, my mother, she would just throw it away. She say, "Those teachers could help you be somebody, but they ain't gonna." So she didn't care whether I went to school or not. Only when I would hang 'round the house and get on her nerves, she would say, "Hanna, get off your butt and go kill some time at the school house." So I would go and hang out in the yard or the locker room or whatever.

I cain't read no label on no bottle of medicine. I cain't fill out no forms, and I cain't read no notices. So the way I saw it, the school failed me. Why should I give them a second chance to fail my own kids? That's why I didn't knock myself out to get them to school some days. I only bothered to get them there if I wanted to get them out from under my feet all day long.

Now—now it's different. I feel like I am a partner with the school. They helped me to see that it could go either way for my kids. They could wind up on the streets like I did, or they could make somethin' of their self. But I got to show them that school is important. 'Cause if they see that I don't care, then they ain't gonna care either.

When I began to feel that someone at B. F. Day care about us, then I began to care, too, and that's why I am a partner with the teachers and the principal. I feel good about myself now, and I feel good about the school. That make a big difference in my kid's attitude about learnin' and gettin' along with the teachers and the other students.

LOST CASES: WHEN PARENTS REFUSE THE PARTNERSHIP

The early, negative home/school conflict that Hanna described, which is experienced by many other economically impoverished students, is a phenomenon addressed by such educators as James Comer (1980):

> Children in home–school conflict situations often receive a double message from their parents: "The school is the hope for your future, listen, be good and learn" and "the school is your enemy." The latter message can be driven home in a very subtle way: "Mrs. Jones yelled at you because she doesn't like us." On the other hand, in a school in which the staff and community are in harmony, the parent's response to the same complaint might be, "Mrs. Jones scolded you when you didn't finish your work because she wants you to do well in school." Children who receive the "school is the enemy" message often go after the enemy—act up, undermine the teacher, undermine the school program, or otherwise exercise their veto power.... the power not to learn, not to attend, not to behave well. (pp. 30, 27)

To be sure, although estrangement between home and school may be quite different from place to place, the very existence of a negative struggle for power can result only in a child's sense that no one cares whether or not he or she attends classes. At some point, the child must then question his or her own self-worth and value.

Nine-year-old Jessie, a student at B. F. Day for the last three months, manifested a negative home/school conflict as she wet and soiled her pants in class at the start of each day and responded to her teacher's efforts to help by stating, "My mother say you a white pig and she shit on you." A visit to Jessie's home revealed a daily struggle for survival that staggered even a vivid imagination.

The bedroom windows of the street-level apartment looked out at a sidewalk strewn with garbage overflowing from four rusted and dented trash cans. Just to the right of these bedroom windows stood the remains of an ill-fitted building entrance door missing several hinges, doorknob, window pane, and street number. This remnant of what once was swung open on one top hinge, revealing hallway walls covered with graffiti, cracked and pitted, linoleum floors, and mailboxes lacking doors. Perhaps most appalling was the stench of a dead rat lying just under the mailboxes. Only that rancid smell could distract me from the sight of hundreds of roaches moving along every square foot of space. Just past the mailboxes was the doorway to Apartment 1A, residence of Beatrice and her two daughters, Pearl and Jessie.

Beatrice opened the door wearing what appeared to be a man's trousers and shoes. A stained blouse was tied at her waist. Beatrice's welcome was brief as she returned to her kitchen to continue defrosting her refrigerator freezer.

A half-painted yellow table, once brown, was surrounded by upholstered chairs whose exposed stuffing and wobbly legs showed their age. There was clutter everywhere—soiled plates and cups, old newspapers, empty beer bottles, unopened junk mail, a can of shaving cream. It all seemed to blend into chaos. Beatrice chopped at the ice with a butcher knife as she talked about her unmet needs:

> What I want is a refrig that don' have to be chopped. You know, like the freezer don' get all that white ice. When I was back in Newark, I had that what you call no-frost job. O' course I was livin' with a dude, so I could live better than now.

Beatrice's 3-year-old daughter, Pearl, wrapped her arms around her mother's thigh and seemed to mark the spot as a cat would by brushing her cheek lightly against the trousers. The paucity of personal space in this crowded living area led Beatrice to slap Pearl across the face. "What I tell you 'bout touchin' me when I choppin' my fridge. Can' but find a spot for my own self, so you think I wan' you slobberin' all over me?" Beatrice seemed pensive for a moment. "What that smell. Did you soil in your pants?" Pearl began to wail as she cautiously moved away from Beatrice. But her mother got in one last swat across Pearl's behind. "You stink. Now get away from me and lay over there away from where I can smell you." Beatrice resumed her conversation in an angry tone of voice:

> Okay, so what you wan' to know about KOOL-IS? 'Cause I tell you this: That school [B. F. Day] ain't been nothin' but trouble for me. They be callin' the child abuse and all that business. They think 'cause they help me get a couple beds and a piece a ole couch that I owe them. I don' owe nobody. I found this apartment by myself when I come up this way. My sister, she help me find this place. The school only give me the beds and that piece a ole couch by that steam pipe. What the school say? I bet they say

they gave me that steam pipe, too, right? That the way it be with people like me. When you colored, you get a steam pipe. The thing is, it don' give no steam. We be freezin' here in the winter. That what I be sayin'. I got ice in the fridge. I got ice on the pipe. Let the school get me a frost-free job. I ain' interested in nothin' else.

Last week a man got it with double barrels right in the chest right in front my window. He be dealin' [in drugs] and get what comin' to him. But my kids see everything. They be playin' on the stoop. So I tell them to get in here. Then I call the police. They come quick, but the dude already dead. I can' think 'bout these things or I go crazy. You tell Miss Preston that I need a frost-free. My sister, at least she got a frost-free in her place. When I get that, I talk 'bout Jessie.

Beatrice's story was only one of many that might fall into the category of "lost cases," as Janet Preston later described them:

Mind you, I said, "lost cases," *not* "lost causes." Just because some homeless mothers are not responsive to KOOL-IS does not mean that we should trash the entire program or our good intentions.

I never said KOOL-IS was one big success story. For every small victory, we experience many overwhelming defeats. But as with anything worthwhile in life, you have to risk and accept failure in order to attain success. Every parent is an individual and must be provided with the same opportunity for success as any other parent. Whether they move on the opportunity to improve their own life and that of their child is a whole other issue. That's the way it is with the KOOL-IS program.

EFFORTS IN COLLABORATION

In order to generate and sustain open discourse between home and school, the attitude at B. F. Day is that the parent is equally as important a target of positive intervention as is the student. "Parents who have missed a first chance at education have the opportunity to experience a renaissance ... in their own educational lives," one veteran teacher of 20 years stated exuberantly. For example, Gabrielle, a young mother of four, was given the opportunity to work with a first-grader who "showed signs of emotional stress during classroom reading instruction." The uniqueness of the arrangement lay in the fact that Gabrielle could not read; therefore, she was perceived by the school as an equally important target for academic intervention. Gabrielle shared her story:

> Once, I say to this little chil', "I never learn to read too good, so I don' know how I can help you. I think maybe I more scared o' books than you is." Well, this sweet little boy climb up my lap, and he be sayin' just like this, "I teach you how to read. I tell you what my teacher say. Then, you tell me what she mean. Then, we both learn the readin'. Then, we don' be scared o' books no more." I tell you, I never thought the day would come, but we both be readin' now. The Lord work in strange ways. Almost as strange as the angels in this school buildin'. You never know what ideas these teachers gonna come up with next.

In this way, Gabrielle had the opportunity to partake in both a growth and learning experience while, at the same time, contributing to the emotional well-being of a small child.

Of course, those that are economically depleted are not necessarily emotionally or educationally depleted. One-time homeless moms can nurture, cuddle, advise, tutor, supervise, cook, bake, and carry out an assortment of other successful activities at school. Janet oversees such projects by making the necessary arrangements with classroom teachers. Each parent at B. F. Day has the opportunity to experience not only "a sense of altruism" but, equally as important, "a quickening sense of learning" (Sarason, 1977, p. 40).

Establishing rapport and enlisting children and parents in their own care is primary to the emotional and social growth that ensues over weeks and sometimes months. At this school, assumptions and generalizations about the impoverished as "a class of people" are dispelled, and communication is shared by individuals who are culturally and developmentally quite different.

EMPOWERMENT THROUGH CHOICE AND DECISION MAKING

Trust and warm, personal relationships develop within a structured environment as school personnel provide each student and parent with a sense of empowerment through choice and decision making. Working together on classroom and larger school projects permits teacher and parent to become better acquainted in an informal and personal way. What begins as a "sense of welcome" on the part of visiting and participating parents soon evolves into a "sense of belonging" and affil-

iation. As is the case with most human relationships, when social alienation and estrangement are replaced with friendship, the seeds of sharing and bonding take root for both teacher and parent.

Sometimes these relationships must be adjusted along the way
because, even in this school's unusual emotional climate, traditional
attitudes can linger. Fine (1993) has pointed out the dangers:

> In scenes in which power asymmetries are not addressed and hierarchical
> bureaucracies are not radically transformed, parents end up looking indi-
> vidually "needy," "naive," or "hysterical" and appear to be working in
> opposition to teachers.... Rarely do they have the opportunity to work col-
> laboratively with educators inventing what could be a rich, engaging, and
> democratic system for public education. (p. 685)

Estelle, mother of five boys, perceived such a potential problem and
creatively transformed a power asymmetry into a true collaboration. She
narrated her initial experience with a teacher at B. F. Day:

> As soon as my son's teacher sent home a note requesting my help
> in planning a field trip, I stopped still in my tracks. I felt I had to
> establish my role clear and fast. The question was: Did the teacher
> really want me to help in planning with a capital P, or did she
> want me to hang out at the back of the line and make sure we
> didn't lose any kids. I would have been more than glad to act as a
> chaperon, but I wanted the teacher to be honest and not try to
> pull one over on me with this "planning" business.
>
> Let's get real here. The teacher is educated and I'm not, so
> why should she be interested in what I think about her class field
> trip? Well, it turned out that she wanted a chaperon. We talked
> about it, and I asked her to please put her cards on the table the
> next time she needed me. Because this was like asking me to
> serve on the parent council when in reality I was only going to
> serve coffee and cake.
>
> I may not be a college grad, but I am not naive. She was a
> college grad, but she was behaving in a naive way. Once we got
> past the surface stuff, we got to know each other real well. Now
> we work together all the time—as one thinking individual to
> another. I make decisions and she makes decisions, but we under-
> stand each other from the word "go."

At B. F. Day, power symmetry and collaboration are the ideals that
support the sometimes uncomfortable process of adjustment. The great
reward to parent and school is the strength of the bond.

CHAPTER 11

Life at Benjamin Franklin Day

In September 1991, Carole, her staff, and more than 300 students returned to the newly renovated B. F. Day. Construction workers were still on the site, and their work was quickly turned into a new curriculum. Children learned about carpentry, masonry, plumbing, roofing, electrical wiring, painting, and teamwork. Supervised by a gardener, they planted flowers, shrubs, and seeds. This fascinating new environment was a concrete affirmation of a more hopeful vision of what life could be like at the school.

Actual implementation of socialized reforms at B. F. Day had already begun to have remarkable consequences. According to data obtained from Bill James at C-STARS, 71 students and their families received comprehensive services at B. F. Day during the early stages of KOOL-IS from September 1989 through June 1990. From September 1990 through June 1991, 64 students and their families were serviced; 53 students and their families were served between September 1991 and January 1992. Data obtained in January 1990 showed that while the student population of B. F. Day as a whole was composed of 53% minority students, 86% of the homeless children served by KOOL-IS were from African-American, Native American, or Hispanic families. Single female parents headed 87% of the homeless families. Children served averaged 8.2 years in age.

During their two-year stay at John Hay, teachers had begun to focus on the affective aspects of learning, supporting both the social and emotional growth of their students. In some cases, teachers had comfortably begun to act as "parent surrogates" (Comer, 1988). As the staff came to understand that learning takes place in relationships, and that children very much want to please the "significant adults" in their lives, the students began to show marked improvement in academic achievement and socialization. The climate for learning was set.

On a Thursday afternoon, I watched a class of 21 laughing, chat-

103

Jo Daly, music teacher: "I realized that, as a teacher, the love that I felt for each child had to be unconditional."

tering third-graders as they walked, single-file, down the corridor after a lunch and recess period. Each child appeared to be sharing the excitement of lunch hour with another child. The classroom teacher, following the group, called to the class leader and motioned that he come to a halt. The class gradually quieted down, in anticipation of what was about to come. On a hand signal from the teacher, each child entered the classroom and found his or her seat. The unity of behavior observed during the first two procedural and directional segments of the day's math lesson suggested that the children had learned which behaviors were suitable, appropriate, and expected in the classroom. In this way, "environmental competence" was fostered, diminishing the chances for "learned helplessness" (Steele, 1973). It was wonderful to see this order and calm in the same school in which, so short a time ago, chaos was the rule.

An articulate, formerly homeless 9-year-old who was watering windowsill plants took the time to describe to me the sense of social competence and empowerment he had achieved as he learned to assume responsibility for his choices and actions:

> I used to push and shove a lot. And I used to throw chairs and tables at the other kids. But I don't make bad choices so much no more. If you make a bad choice, then you need to think about what you done and what the consequences be. Then a big person will help you to figure out why you made a bad choice. Then tomorrow is a new day, and you got a new chance to make a good choice.
>
> Anyway, I want to get a coupon for a free hug from my teacher or the principal. If I make a good choice, I get a good consequence. I can get a hug and maybe a kiss on my cheek. I could save up my hug coupons and get lots and lots and lots of hugs on the same day. That be real good.
>
> If you make a bad choice, that don't mean you be a bad person. Everyone makes a bad choice sometimes. You ought to listen to Mrs. Williams. She the principal of this whole big school and she make bad choices sometimes, but that don't mean she be a bad person. 'Cause she feel sorry, and she try her best not to do the same bad choice again.
>
> The principal, Mrs. Williams, say she no different from me. She got good days, and she got bad days. I got good days, and I got bad days. She make a bad choice sometimes, and so do I. Mrs. Williams say we the same because we both good people and we both make mistakes. But the next day we could make a good choice....
>
> You in charge of your own self. You in charge of your own

choices, and you in charge of your own consequences. If you be unhappy with your own consequences, then you better make good choices tomorrow.

Critical to understanding the changes in this child's thinking and behavior is the recognition of an underlying change in role relationships between teachers and students as well as principal and students at B. F. Day. Very early on, it was acknowledged that children could no more be ordered or lectured to change their ways in interacting with the world than could their teachers. As was the case with professional staff, cognitive and behavioral change on the part of students required that they be active participants in the process of changing the emotional and social climate within the school. Each student was treated as someone whose opinion mattered. When the views of students were solicited in the establishment of school rules and codes of conduct, an implicit message was conveyed that they could and did influence the social and cultural climate of school life.

Addressing issues of student socialization, Brophy's (1991) comment supports the observed changes at B. F. Day:

> Consistent projection of positive expectations, attributions, and social labels to the students is important in fostering positive self-concepts and related motives that orient the students toward prosocial behavior.... Students who are consistently treated as if they are well-intentioned individuals who respect themselves and others and desire to act responsibly, morally, and prosocially are more likely to live up to those expectations and acquire those qualities than students who are treated as if they had the opposite qualities. (p. 218)

More often than not, a young child perceives behavior as an activity directed by outside influences and authoritative figures, such as parents and teachers. Assuming responsibility for one's own words and actions fosters a clearer understanding that individual behavior is actually an independent choice. When the teacher offers the child alternatives and points out that the choice of behavior is his or her own, an opportunity to make consistent connections between cause and effect is created within a nonjudgmental atmosphere.

Over time, the teachers at B. F. Day came to recognize that psychological intimidation of defiant students through verbal denouncement and exclusionary tactics, although effective for the moment, was extremely harmful to both the students' self-esteem and the bond of trust between teacher and student over the long haul. This recognition led to discussions of better methods of discipline. Situations were devised in which a disruptive child could cool down with the help of an adult (often the principal, another teacher, social worker, case manager, or volunteer parent) either in the transition room, social worker's office, or library. This "significant adult" would attempt to help the child come up with alternative ways of handling his or her frustration. Giving the child an immediate opportunity to "talk out" the problem and "work through" better ways of handling the situation that initially incited the outburst conveyed an implicit vote of adult confidence that the child could exhibit self-control and discover a better means of conflict resolution. In this way, children could gracefully return to class while avoiding the humiliation that often accompanies public loss of control and disciplinary action in the classroom setting. As Comer (1980) has commented, "When feelings and actions can be put into words, fear and anxiety can be reduced and the world seems to come under greater personal control" (p. 173).

Comer's point is well-reflected in the emotive assertion of one troubled 11-year-old student:

Hey, if I let some good lookin' woman boss me around in the classroom all day, how am I supposed to feel macho? At my home and in my streets, I got to have machismo, or I am nobody. My mother, she depends on me to be the man in our house 'cause her ole man, he nothin' but a drunken bum. So what am I supposed to tell her? Should I tell her I'm a sissy in the classroom? Should I tell her I can't go to work at night 'cause I got homework? No way, man. I got to survive on the streets. I got to collect the bets for the bookies. I got to slash tires if the scumbags don't pay up their losses. You know how much I get to slash a couple tires? More than you make workin' in McDonalds, that's for sure. So you see I can't worry about what no teacher think 'cause she don't understand about me or my life.

This story was not new to his teacher. She told me she had heard it many times in the past:

It is life in the slums. He is not the problem; his behavior and lifestyle are the issues to be addressed. If he learns his times table—well, fine. But more important, he has to discover his niche in society, and in order to do that he has to be heard and understood. He needs to be accepted where he is at, not necessarily where I want him to be. It's October. I've got eight months to reach him. If he believes that I truly care about him and understand his personal baggage, he will let me be a positive influence in his life.

The cultural ethos at B. F. Day fosters the belief that criticism must be focused on words, ideas, and actions—never people. When teachers supplant verbal and nonverbal "putdowns" with strong "buildups," a sense of trust begins to develop. I saw many instances of counselor-like approaches as principal and teachers dealt with students who had committed some infraction of school rules. They often reflected a humanistic philosophy in the way they listened to each child's problems and presented alternative perspectives, behaviors, and values for the child's consideration.

SHARING THE CLASSROOM

Within each of the nine classrooms I observed, there seemed to be a meshing of work and friendship that produced a sense of integration and intimacy among all students, regardless of gender, color, or economic status. Small faces represented faraway places: Vietnam, Cambodia, Kenya, Ghana, Uganda, Mexico, El Salvador. The very way in which the teachers interacted with the students and exemplified personalized interactions (placing a hand on a child's shoulder, stroking a cheek, patting a back, or simply maintaining eye contact and lovingly squeezing the shoulders of a child experiencing frustration) seemed to foster and reinforce a sense of rootedness and affiliation.

I saw this illuminating sense of social support over and over again as students engaged in various activities at various times with each other. In crucial contrast to the classrooms observed by Rist (1970), who discussed their "microethnography," no "'social distance' was maintained between the various strata of the society as represented by the children" (p. 444). Racial overtones were never evidenced as the teachers almost imperceptibly encouraged the intermingling of different socioeconomic groups through pairing, seating arrangement, and delegated group assignments. As Grannis (1967) has poignantly stated:

> Every school represents to its students a model of society and its possibilities. In the very composition of the students and teachers,… in the ways that people talk with one another, learn and work and play together, and in the expectations the school holds for its students—in all these ways, and more, the school instructs about society." (p. 17)

All classrooms at the refurbished B. F. Day reflected a comfortable and familial environment that afforded a sense of home and security for all students. Bright colors, interesting shapes, and a variety of textures appeared on the folding screens that divided spaces, on closet doors, and on chalkboards. The children's compositions and accompanying artwork as well as bound booklets and sculpted constructions appeared in every nook and cranny. It was clear that each classroom belonged to the children in residence. As Proshansky and Wolfe (1975) have observed:

> The bulletin board which says "Our Best Paintings" all too often relects the teacher's idea of what "best" really is in terms of an adult's sense of beauty. Indeed, the well-manicured room and bulletin boards are often telltale evidence of whose room this really is. (p. 34)

Within each classroom at B. F. Day, the children have been given the opportunity to impose their "aesthetic criteria" over a period of time in order to create an atmosphere pleasing to them. In assuming this responsibility, the children have an opportunity to "see themselves as having greater functional importance within the setting and having greater functional identity" (Moos, 1974, p. 10).

One third-grade teacher described the reality of the classroom quite eloquently:

> The lack of permanence in each homeless child's situation permeates the core of his very being. There is no order or constancy or logic in their daily existence. They are the youngest and most vulnerable victims of status abuse across society. The classroom is perhaps their only retreat into a microcosm where they are in control of their destiny and where they are heard—their laughter, their tears, their anguish. Everyone needs a place to rest their head and feel loved. Everyone needs a special place to store their personal belongings and memories. At B. F. Day, we provide such a place within the classroom.

The countless number of posted child-written messages or letters that were less than two weeks old was an illuminating and salient statement regarding what Ahola-Sidaway (1988) has described as the "sense of rootedness the children experienced at a very personal level" (p. 8):

> James will you meet me in the playground during lunch. I brought a picture of the dog I used to have before we moved to the shelter. His name is Duffy. I don't know where he is no more.
>
> Lester

Dear Lester,
We kood make copees of the pichure you got and then we kood
poste it on the stors and then sum lady kood find Duffy. Then we
kood hide him in the hotele.

James

P.S. Don be sad cose I help you find Duffy

Within each of these posted notes, there seemed to be an understood dialogue between the writer and the expected reader. A closer look
often reflected a second dialogue, or compassionate monologue, which
the writer seemed to be carrying on in his own mind. This opportunity
to express thoughts on paper led to a greater sphere within which he
could effect change through wise choices and actions.

The teacher was the key person in effectively coordinating, facilitating, and coaching instruction within the classroom. Assignment patterns appeared to be tailored to create the opportunity for student
autonomy and initiative. Each classroom might best be described as
"multidimensional," in that a wide variety of congruent and related
activities all occurred simultaneously.

Portable partitions were used to bound various activity areas. This
adaptive strategy enhanced the independent work of those children
engrossed in a single project, while still allowing for mobility and conversation among students working in pairs or small groups. Thus the
children could change their personal space and interpersonal relationships in each segment of any particular task.

Another salient feature of each classroom was the teacher's ability
to shift the program to suit a particular child's cognitive capacity at a
given moment. Each student's itinerary was modified to the pace at
which he or she worked most comfortably. Flexibility and rationality
appeared to guide teachers in their choice of the tasks and responsibilities to be shouldered by each child. And without a doubt, visual, audi-
tory, gestural, and verbal communication between each child and
teacher afforded an equal opportunity for success regardless of color,
hairstyle, or dress.

PERSONAL SPACE AND SOCIAL INTERACTION

A homeless child often has problems with his or her personal space, that
space with invisible boundaries into which intruders may not come.
Invasion of these invisible boundary lines is often perceived as an intru-
sion into one's safety and a violation of one's territory. The following

scenario exemplifies this problem, which often erupts in the classroom.

Ricardo had found a corner in which to write a story about a book he had read over the weekend. Suddenly, he raised his voice in order to inform his teacher that "Michael stole the seat." In so doing, "Michael touched me [Ricardo] with his shoulder and knee." Ricardo then directed numerous hostile remarks toward Michael, regarding his perception of this spatial invasion of privacy. "I am involved in a very private story. I don't need [Michael] crowding in on me and reading my stuff." Michael attempts to explain, saying he had "just tried to move an empty chair." "I was just trying to get this chair over to the science table 'cause there ain' no more chair over there. When I try to move it, my shoulder bump into Ricardo's shoulder. He kicked out his leg so my knee touch him. What he so touchy about? What's his problem?" Ricardo's gesture, posture, and choice of location were meant to convey a clear meaning that Michael apparently did not pick up on. Ricardo had situated himself in such a way that a room partition shielded one side of him and a vacant chair on which he rested his novel remained on the other side of him.

According to Sommer (1969), "In many situations defense of personal space is so entangled with defense of an immediate territory that one sees them as part of a single process—the defense of privacy—that involves fundamental questions of space usage and property rights" (p. 45). Ricardo chose to describe Michael's physical contact as "crowding in on [him]." This episode seemed to represent the defense of both physical and psychological space—in essence, the defense of life space. In the case of homeless children, sensitivity to crowding is experienced in both a salient and negative way as less and less space seems available, whether in a shelter or welfare hotel (Kozol, 1985).

Yolanda Gonzalez, an insightful and innovative third- and fourth-grade teacher, reflected the staff's new insight that children who were cooped up in one small motel room all afternoon and evening would have great difficulty remaining in the confinement of their school seats for long periods of time. Moreover, those students residing in shelters that were large and noisy barracks-like structures would not think twice about speaking out of turn or calling across the room. As for the children who had homes, ways were devised to enlighten and educate them about the life experiences of the homeless by way of stories, films, and speakers.

Enlightened teachers began to help all students learn the school's culture—its moral values, educational expectations, accepted codes of dress and behavior, and ground rules for social interaction. Student responsibility in exercising novel problem-solving and conflict-resolution skills was clearly an integral part of the school's ethos. In establishing the tone for an effective learning climate, B. F. Day children were given the opportunity to expand their repertoire of positive and productive life experiences.

COMBATING THE STATUS QUO

All children enter school wanting to learn, yet children of color begin to resist school sometime along the way to higher education (Grant, 1989). Teachers at B. F. Day seemed well aware of this fact as they discussed and enacted strategies to combat this trend, often highly evident in schools serving large numbers of poverty-afflicted children.

First and foremost, at B. F. Day, students' learning difficulties were not attributed to their socioeconomic status. Living conditions, single-parent households, welfare dependency, parental drug abuse: These were not considered personal characteristics or traits of individual children, but rather life circumstances. Effective teachers viewed their students' academic problems as something to be corrected. Low achievement was not considered a student-owned problem, thus releasing the teacher from responsibility to effect change. On the contrary, identified low achievers received extensive and repeated one-on-one explanations about the purpose of instructional activities and the reasons that mastering a task would prove useful in their everyday lives.

Moreover, all students were encouraged to tell teachers when something did not make sense to them. Teachers showed students how they themselves performed a task (e.g., locating a subject within the index of a book or the proper use of a thesaurus), and this demonstration often imparted a readiness skill for an activity.

The enacted aspects of academic curriculum, instruction, and grouping for children of poverty did not appear to differ markedly from those rendered in the school as a whole. Across classrooms, children of varying ability were intermingled through cooperative and team-learning interactions in order to achieve "blended grouping." Enlightened by current educational theory, teachers seemed determined to avoid fixed, long-term ability grouping (Slavin, 1989). There appeared to be a proportionately greater focus on learner attributes than on presumed learner deficits. Respect for the cultural and linguistic backgrounds of all students seemed to foster active and inquiring participation, rather than a passive receptiveness, on the part of ethnic minorities. Analytic thinking and communicative skills were encouraged in all children, most particularly those who demonstrated severe dialect speech patterns and limited exposure to print. In these ways, teachers were able to transcend stereotypic ideas and misconceptions about the "disadvantaged learner," and in so doing minimize their risk of academic misdiagnoses.

FEATURES OF CURRICULUM AND
INSTRUCTIONAL APPROACHES

Through both interviews and direct classroom observation, it became clear to me that B. F. Day teachers were aware of those instructional features that often undermine learning, particularly in classrooms that serve large numbers of non-standard-English-speaking students. Teacher-controlled instruction was balanced with equal opportunities for self-direction and self-pacing during student-controlled segments of engaged time on task. Redundant rote and drill practices in workbooks or on ditto sheets were markedly outnumbered by novel tasks in which teacher and student engaged in direct discourse about the subject matter. Across classrooms, teachers avoided fixed sequential and linear mastery of "the basics," so that the more challenging critical and communicative skills were not postponed unnecessarily.

Such classroom practices are supported by researchers who believe that too many at-risk children continue to practice unmastered basic decoding skills year after year. These children receive minimal instruction; they never learn the vital comprehension strategies of interpreting and constructing meaning (Garcia, Jimenez, & Pearson, 1989). Across most school settings on most school days, low achievers are often found working alone on repetitive, low-level tasks. This so-called individualized instruction minimizes the time available for more effective teacher-led group instruction (Broikou, Allington, & Jachym, 1989; McGill-Franzen & Allington, 1990). "Much of what is done to low achievement children in schools is done in the name of 'individual needs,' but less of this addresses an individual child's needs than we might expect" (Allington, 1991, pp. 17–18).

Slow readers in classrooms across the country tend to be engaged in round-robin oral readings, where errors in decoding are monitored and corrected by peers and teacher (Applebee, Langer, & Mullis, 1988). Using this approach, nonnative English pronunciation is often misinterpreted as a symptom of decoding problems or even as a language deficit (Goodman, Watson, & Burke, 1987). Opportunities for developing fluency and self-correction skills are limited. In addition, these children need to think less about what they are reading, as their teachers tend to ask fewer comprehension questions than they do of faster readers (Moll, Estrada, Diaz, & Lopes, 1980).

In contrast, B. F. Day classroom reading instruction featured a focus on development of comprehension strategies. Group discussion of the author's purpose, the drawing of inferences, and the summarization of themes were highlighted, following silent readings of culturally familiar stories. Teachers commented that off-task behavior prevailed less in the regular classroom than in the resource room; therefore every effort was made to keep slower readers from remedial room segregation. This observation of and approach to slow achievers is supported by the research of Haynes and Jenkins (1986) as well as that of Allington and McGill-Franzen (1989).

MEANINGFUL LEARNING

Meaningful writing is valued at B. F. Day as a form of empowerment and as a means of creative expression. Writing is used as a tool to teach students how to think more effectively as they express opinions, moods, aspirations, and complaints—or merely pose questions. The writing of students speaking black English is considered part of their primary language system or ethnic dialect (Farr Whiteman, 1980). Dialect-based differences in writing are respected rather than judged as errors. Regarding spelling, a lack of mastery is not taken as an indication that a child is unprepared to write stories. Invented spelling and a whole-language approach support children's initial attempts to put pen to paper.

The mathematics achievement of racial and ethnic minorities (excluding Asian-Americans) across the country reflects a gross divergence from the national average, a divergence that grows wider in higher grades (Dossey, Mullis, Lindguist, & Chambers, 1988). This disparity has been attributed to the widespread practice of waiting to give children the opportunity to engage in conceptual problem-solving activities until they have demonstrated mastery of low-level computation skills. For example, the inability of a student to memorize the multiplication tables may lead to repeated workbook exercises, with little instructional time given to analytical thinking skills (Peterson, 1988). Children of poverty tend to enter school less prepared, than their middle-class peers to attain computational skills. Consequently, the introduction of critical-thinking and problems-solving skills is postponed for them—sometimes until they reach high school, when it often is too late. To combat the problem, B. F. Day teachers emphasized sustained discourse about mathematical ideas and applications between students and teacher and among students, as suggested in recent studies (Russell & Friel, 1989).

In tailoring each child's learning experience to his or her individual and special needs, capabilities, and potential, B. F. Day teachers have greatly improved the academic performance of all children. In 1993, B. F. Day students ranked 38th among all 65 Seattle elementary schools in academic performance—a strong contrast to their position as the lowest-ranked school in 1989. As B. F. Day draws students from all over the city, indeed from around the world, it is not surprising that 16 foreign languages are the primary languages among almost a quarter of its students. It is to the credit of the faculty that such potential language barriers have not impeded learning on any level.

B. F. Day teachers believe that there are as many gifted and talented children of every race, culture, and economic situation as there are average or learning-disabled children. With this in mind, and with the support of in-service training, teachers consciously and deliberately monitor their own behaviors that might sustain the poor performance of low achievers (Good & Biddle, 1988) and result in minimal movement from lower to upper tracks (Oakes, 1985).

As Goodlad (1979) has pointed out:

> We can talk about healthy schools in much the same way we talk about healthy people. Schools are like living organisms, with characteristics that can be described in varying degrees as healthy or unhealthy. Schools, as culture, must assume responsibility for their health and be held accountable. (p. 73)

This, in fact, is the case at B. F. Day. There is a sense of health and wholeness that pervades every aspect of school life. Teachers, students, and parents have a sense of belonging to a special place. To this end, B. F. Day offers an extraordinary educative environment, in a place often called "The Family School."

CHAPTER 12

Emergent Themes

The case of Benjamin Franklin Day Elementary School suggests that such multivariate risk factors as childhood poverty, family chaos, chronic stress, and psychological vulnerability reinforce one another to cause subversive social behavior, learning problems, and, ultimately, school failure. The plight of children exposed to these risks increases tenfold when an unsupportive, impersonal, and deprecatory school experience compounds the destructive effects of an unstable homelife. Conversely, when deliberate social action on the part of principal, teachers, and community is coordinated within a psychologically warm, nurturing, and easily accessible environment such as the neighborhood school, the collaborative effort can provide the basis for positive outcomes for manageable problems.

The positive transformation of B. F. Day affirms the research and model programs of enlightened and scholarly educational leaders who are providing rich testimony to the power of responsible family/school/community collaboration in decision making and problem solving (Comer, 1980; Cuban, 1988; Epstein, 1991, Fine, 1993).

REFLECTIONS ON BUREAUCRATIC STRUCTURES

There is a strong consensus that bureaucratic schooling as we know it is the antithesis of collaborative schooling. This provides a compelling rationale for the reconsideration and restructuring of school organization and function in the 1990s. As Linda Darling-Hammond (1990) has stated, "In the final analysis, perfected bureaucracy with its emphasis on developing rules 'without regard for persons' is intrinsically unsuited to the task of educating human beings" (p. 30).

Clark and Meloy (1990) have pointed out that "alternatives to the bureaucratic structure are overwhelmed not by the practicalness of the

Barbara Smith, grandparent and volunteer tutor, and Joe Garcia, former director of the Atlantic Street Center and originator of the KOOL-IS program, greet Carole Williams in the hall.

bureaucratic model but by its omnipresence" and have asked, "How can one imagine operable alternatives to a structure so firmly in place?" (p. 16). They propose that classical bureaucracy as posited by Max Weber laid the groundwork for the organizational structure and function of American institutions, both public and private, and they quote Weber as follows:

> [Bureaucracy by] its specific nature ... develops the more perfectly the more the bureaucracy is "dehumanized," the more completely it succeeds in eliminating from official business love, hatred, and all purely personal, irrational, and emotional elements which escape calculation. This is the specific nature of bureaucracy and it is appraised as its special virtue. (p. 5)

Darling-Hammond (1990) suggests that the logic and strategy behind classical bureaucratic organization and management have infiltrated the process of schooling in rather pronounced ways:

> Schools are agents of government that can be administered by hierarchical decision-making and controls. Policies are made at the top of the system and handed down to administrators who translate them into rules and procedures. Teachers follow the rules and procedures ... and students are processed according to them....
>
> The circular bottom line assumption is that this process, if efficiently administered, will produce the outcomes that the system desires. If the outcomes are not satisfactory, the final assumption is that the prescriptions are not yet sufficiently detailed or the process of implementation is not sufficiently exact. Thus the solutions to educational problems always lie in more precise regulation of educational or management processes....
>
> In this sense the policies embody state-oriented rather than client-oriented control of education. (pp. 27–29)

ALTERNATIVES TO BUREAUCRATIC STRUCTURES

If, in fact, American schools are bureaucracies, then the following train of thought proposed by Clark and Meloy (1990) is essential if we wish to rethink and restructure the roles of principals, teachers, students, parents, and communities in the process of schooling:

> Suppose that one could imagine an organizational structure with the individual as its building block, exhibiting a total regard for persons. Reasonably, this personal model would trade off control for empowerment, domination for freedom, and authority for consent. An organization built on these principles would choose its members and leaders, concern itself with the self-actualization of all its members, share the power tools of the orga-

nization, de-emphasize hierarchical relationships, and create opportunities for self-fulfilling jobs....

Our metaphors for leadership suggest an individual in control, holding onto rather than passing the buck, mobilizing the troops, running a lean and mean organization, making hard decisions, not running a popularity contest. (p. 5)

Like many other educational leaders, Carole struggled against the assumption that "the basic bureaucratic form is the only way in which school systems and schools can be organized" (Clark & Meloy, 1990, p. 9). She not only imagined an organizational structure that valued the worth and self-actualization of the average human being; she created a school culture that knocked down paralyzing assumptions about classes of people and that uprooted managerial strategies that fostered a "mediocrity of the masses." Such an accepting, consenting, and collaborative climate generated self-direction, commitment, and professional growth as teachers quickly learned that prejudices about "people" did not necessarily fit individual "persons," and that pigeonholing "him" and "her" into faceless groups of "them" is truly self-defeating.

Carole's keys to debureaucratization were minimizing hierarchical relationships through empowerment of others, organizing individuals around social problems rather than arbitrary job functions, and breaking through barriers of isolationism perpetuated by organizational compartments and specialization of roles. In choosing to share her authority, Carole transformed her school into a self-actuating lever of social reform, making an indirect impact on the neighborhood in which B. F. Day resides. Her strong belief that reality is not a given, but rather "a mere set of circumstances which can be rearranged," encouraged those around her to exercise self-direction and self-commitment toward attainment of both personal and collective goals and dreams.

LEADERSHIP AND VISION

Carole often talked to her staff about the way things might be if each individual assumed the perspective of another—teacher, student, or parent—even if only for a little while. Sergiovanni (1991) has captured Carole's approach to changing both outlook and attitude on the part of teachers in his insightful discussion about leadership and vision:

Vision is an important dimension of purposing and without it the very point of leadership is missed, but the vision of the school must also reflect the hopes and dreams, the needs and interests, the values and beliefs of everyone who has a stake in the school—teachers, parents, and students. In the end, it is what the school stands for that counts.... A binding and solemn agreement needs to emerge that represents a value system for living together and that provides the basis for decisions and actions. This binding and solemn agreement represents the school's covenant.

When both vision and covenant are present, teachers and students respond with increased motivation and commitment and their performance is beyond expectations. (p. 135)

Etzioni (1988) has made a compelling case for emotion, morality, and social bonds as a source of motivation for teachers that is often heightened by a leader who presents as a moral authority. In the case of B. F. Day, Carole established herself as a genuinely sincere leader with a strong commitment to assume responsibility for homeless children and their families. She was an inspirer of decisions, rather than the sole decision maker. Establishing a consensus on social values and goal setting helped define "what this school stands for and hopes to achieve" and in this way empowered teachers via "problem ownership."

SHARING THE BURDEN

Perhaps the best way to empower the community toward achieving a common purpose is to tap into and harness the help and ingenuity of those adults who directly interact with and influence young children. The study of B. F. Day suggests that the first step in accomplishing this feat is the school principal's willingness to acknowledge his or her own limitations and relinquish the "burden of presumed competence" (Barth, 1990).

In a chapter titled "The Social Realities of Teaching," Lieberman and Miller (1992) quote the reflections of an elementary school teacher on this subject, then share their own thoughts:

"I have never heard another teacher say, 'I have a problem.' You just don't do it. You solve the problem on your own, or you pretend that you don't have one. You never open up to anyone about anything important."

For most teachers in most schools, teaching is indeed a lonely enterprise. With so many people engaged in so common a mission in so compact a space and time, it is perhaps the greatest irony—and the greatest tragedy of teaching—that so much is carried on in self-imposed and professionally sanctioned isolation. (p. 11)

The events at B. F. Day strongly suggest that when the principal relinquishes the burden of presumed competence, when she admits that she needs help, she encourages teachers and other staff members to relinquish their burden and to break out of their isolation and loneliness.

By establishing the groundwork for a "helping network," the principal sets the stage for evoking and sustaining images and expectations of ideal school life. If teachers can openly discuss those things they are unhappy with, they can begin to discuss how they would like things to be. It is at this point that staff development meetings can offer avenues of new thought regarding students, parents, and the role of schooling.

PROVIDING ACCESS TO AND OPPORTUNITIES FOR PROFESSIONAL GROWTH

Within the traditional bureaucratic school, lockstep activities and schedules often prevent both novice and veteran teachers from leaving the isolation of the classroom to join their colleagues for dialogue, deliberation, and debate over new and refreshing ideas. The school-level administrator must assume responsibility for ensuring that teachers are provided with free time to meet. The principal's ingenuity in coordinating opportunities for and access to professional growth experiences will definitively influence the direction of the school as a social organization with interactive and helping networks.

In the case of B. F. Day, the principal arranged with district administrators to obtain funds for large-group student events, which freed teachers from each grade to meet and address the issue of neighborhood poverty and its impact on school life. In addition, by adding 15 minutes each morning to the school day, teachers accrued an added two professional days a month in which sustained dialogue could take place in the legal absence of students. According to Griffin (1988):

> There are time and schedule dimensions of school life that principals can orchestrate to bring about the time and space opportunities for participatory decision making....
>
> Interestingly, there are few instances of shifts in time and schedules that can be observed in large numbers of schools. When such shifts are suggested as reasonable ways to create conditions for working on school issues, including curriculum, the problems associated with altering business as usual come to the forefront of attention. Yet in effective schools, schools where important teaching and learning are taking place, such flexibility is, in fact, a new order of business as usual. This flexibility is essential to promoting school-level deliberation and action that are systematic, ongoing and developmental. (p. 201)

In a discussion of teachers as colleagues, Judith Warren Little (1987) has stated, "To forge a group that lasts through time (and through tough times) and that creates achievement worth celebrating is no small challenge" (p. 186). Breaking traditional orientations toward time and schedule is not enough to ensure that rigorous collaboration will not go awry. As Carole points out, "Teachers are human, just like everyone else. Sometimes they feel inadequate, self-conscious, or in need of proving themselves. Individual confidence is a prerequisite to group trust and rapport."

Organized workgroups require a certain level of camaraderie, interest in solving shared problems, and mentor/learner relations among veteran and novice teachers. Teachers designated as mentors or advisers based on their knowledge and problem-solving orientations and skill are often faced with the "collegial/expert dichotomy" (Goodman & Lieberman, 1985, p. 8). The interest and intensity with which the principal focuses upon this issue may be the deciding factor as to when and how cooperative work becomes a matter of school policy. Supported by time, space, resources, and staff assignments, cooperative ventures have a good chance of arriving at successful outcomes. Above all, teachers are able openly to confront issues of privatism, problem hiding, and the anxiety, uncertainty, and ambivalence that accompany change.

SCHOOLS AS PART OF COMMUNITIES

A major step in breaking the bureaucratic mold is to recognize, as Carole did, that the school can no longer be viewed as a context-free, generic institution. Each school must be viewed in a community context—responsive to the particular and distinct needs of the children and parents—if it is to succeed in its educational mission (Sykes, 1990). Respect for diversity must preface and challenge any and all "best" ways to meet the needs of the student (Comer, 1988; Fullan; 1991; Goodlad, 1979).

The foremost educational question must always be: best for whom, in what real-life community situation, and under what school circumstances? Just as the nuances in the colors of a prismatic arc are affected by the backdrop upon which they reflect, so, too, nuances in the mental health, socioeconomic status, racial composition, and cultural values of a neighborhood are affected by a backdrop of shifting demographic cycles of growth, decay, and regeneration.

If schools are to be viewed in the context of community, then the principal's and teachers' professional knowledge base must include an understanding of daily neighborhood life. Carole encouraged and fostered her teachers' education in the grim details of ghetto living, urging teachers to view life in the streets, shelters, parks, and temporary homes with their own eyes. Although such trips were not mandated, most teachers did in fact accept the responsibility and challenge of learning about the neighborhood. It was this face-to-face encounter with painful ghetto reality that formed a bond of morality and purposeful interaction between and among students, teachers, and parents.

The need to participate visibly and vocally in any change process is as crucial for students and parents as it is for teachers. The fit between school and community may be loosely coupled or tightly knit; but either way, it will be effective, as long as there is a shared sense of direction and commitment, the freedom to consent or dissent, and a reasonable span of time for individuals to confront uncertainty, even when changes in course are voluntary.

As Sarason (1982) has succinctly pointed out, there are no easy-to-follow recipes when it comes to proposals for what schools should do or be. Effective family/school/community networks appear to be the creations of those leaders who choose to probe beneath the surfaces of our society and our schools and who are impelled to think differently than they have been accustomed to in the past.

NETWORKING AND RESOURCE EXCHANGE

In the world of schooling, networking and resource exchange are in many ways interchangeable concepts in search of an opportunity for implementation. Loosely related groups of people with diverse backgrounds, agency affiliations, and work roles can barter goods and services to meet needs and goals. When this kind of resource reciprocation occurs, active participants experience a substantial feeling of community and interrelatedness. Satisfying needs and goals is no longer a problem but rather an opportunity and an open challenge to use limited but existing resources effectively.

Collaboration with a local university can be mutually beneficial. The teachers gain knowledge about the living conditions of socially and economically impoverished families and gain a setting conducive to reflection on feelings of confusion, prejudice, and disillusionment; the university gains the opportunity to observe, record, and study children in the school. The fruitful involvement of B. F. Day with the University of Washington, resulting in the KOOL-IS proposal, affirms the value of such collaborative enterprises between school and university.

But the university resource is all too often ignored, even though ample guidelines are available in the literature. The Baldwin-King program initiated in Connecticut in 1968, when the New Haven school system successfully joined forces with the Yale Child Study Center, was surely a landmark case. In their work, clinicians and educators used the knowledge of social and behavioral sciences and education to overcome poor motivation, low self-esteem, discipline problems, and serious learning disabilities in an inner-city school where interpersonal tensions among staff, parents, and students resounded in many ways (Comer, 1980). In light of the fact that there are more than 16,000 school districts across this nation, it is a sad commentary that more than 25 years later, collaboration between universities and schools remains a relatively haphazard occurrence.

Networking with a local social service agency can provide the school with a cadre of social workers or case managers who then have the opportunity to learn about and develop a state-of-the-art formula for successful case management while they coordinate such services as family counseling, health, housing, public welfare, and employment training and then track client progress over an extended period of time. B. F. Day's affiliation with the Atlantic Street Center demonstrates an effective interagency collaboration between a public school and a social service agency.

Finally, the institutionalization of a community and/or parent volunteer cadre of school workers allows for yet another type of individual/interagency collaboration. In *Human Services and Resource Networks* (1977), Sarason stated:

> [Institutions] might gain more resources by developing ways whereby "outside people" normally unconnected with the agency would be given learning experiences productive to their own growth at the same time they were contributing to the setting. (p. 40)

When parents and neighborhood residents are given the opportunity to work as equal partners with school personnel, they develop a sense of being valued not only for who they are but for who they can be. However, equal partnership between school and home depends on the willingness of school personnel to share power. Parents must feel comfortable in volunteer, paid, governance, or management positions if they are not to be merely token members of school committees (Epstein, 1991; Fine, 1993).

THE IMPACT OF NETWORKING

Networking—whether between school and university, school and social service agency, or school and members of the community—has a significant impact on the psychological and social well-being and development of the child, and it also improves family life in indirect ways. When the best elements of human nature rise above the oppressiveness of societal institutions, we can "make each one of our schools an embryonic community life." (Dewey, 1899). In a manner not unlike that of John Dewey, Jane Addams, and Harold Rugg, who were intrigued with the idea of a "school-centered community" that was to house social agencies in order to resolve local economic and ethnic issues, Carole pursued a philosophy of reconstructionism as she altered the social climate, philanthropic attitude, and collective vision and purpose within B. F. Day.

Carole's experience with severely impoverished children and their families sharpened her repudiation of the educational system as one which perpetuates the lifestyle patterns that prevail in a given community. She sought out social networks to transform her school into a multifaceted service agency committed to meeting the needs of the whole child and his or her family.

Comer (1980) has affirmed the value of social networks in realizing a "school-centered community" in today's society, just as it existed in yesterday's towns:

> Tight-knit social networks of approving and disapproving people are more effective determinants of a child's behavior than laws, policemen, security, and surveillance equipment. Eventually the attitudes, values, and behavior of the adult authority figures become a part of a child's character.
>
> Because parents and friends belonging to church and other social networks before the 1940's were related in one way or another to larger community networks, most people reinforced the accepted community standards. The school, the principal, and the staff were an intimate and highly respected part of the social networks of most families. Their authority was an extension of parental authority. Even the school building was hallowed ground. (p. 10)

CHAPTER 13

Recommendations for the Future

Although B. F. Day is "a work in the making," it is a valuable demonstration of how the voices of ordinary individuals can resound in victory, as one school and one community share in a vision of how life might be different for its children. The fact that this school's program is unusual should not minimize its significance. As Lisbeth Schorr (1988) has pointed out, model programs prove that "something can be done to address certain seemingly intractable social problems" and offer us "a benchmark for judging other efforts" (p. 266).

QUESTIONS FOR FUTURE RESEARCH

As Darling-Hammond (1990) has succinctly stated:

> The basic problem in public education today is finding a way to meet the diverse needs of students who come to school with varying capabilities, learning styles, psychological predispositions, family situations, and beliefs about themselves and about what school means for them. Recent concerns about "at-risk" youth—those who drop out, tune out, become pregnant, fall behind—converge with major changes in the home backgrounds of students; more children live in poverty, with one or no parents, in divorced or reconstituted families than ever before in recent history....
>
> These goals and challenges require that schools develop the capacity to meet students' needs and society's demand in a way that they have not before been asked to do. (p. 26)

In attempting to consider the social conditions of poverty and homelessness, future research studies might focus on the school as both a social and an educational service agency. Perhaps the most logical place to begin study would be on the grounds of B. F. Day. In the words of Sarason (1977): "The social soil into which an individual attempts to

126

Seattle business executive Bill Euster (l.) and retired attorney Leo
Anderson (r.) volunteer in a variety of ways to assist B. F. Day and the
community: "Who is 'society' if not you and me?"

plant and nurture the seeds of change is undoubtedly fateful for what will grow. To underestimate the significance of this factor borders on the ridiculous" (p. 186).

Currently, one can only conjecture whether the seeds of change planted by Carole Williams will continue to sprout new shoots and buds each year, producing a fruitful harvest, or rather lose their viability within an ever-changing social soil. The lives of staff, children, and parents who currently comprise the social soil and economic strata of both school and surrounding community are constantly shifting. At the present time, the future development and growth of the KOOL-IS program and the school's other unique programs can only be left to one's imagination. But with the passing of time, future researchers may find it a challenging and engaging pursuit to examine the course of one principal's legacy.

Carole has demonstrated unique leadership ability within concomitant roles as "mandate-bearer" (i.e., top-down agent of change) and "creator of bottom-up reform" (Marsh & Bowman, 1988). Some of her colleagues believe that the effectiveness of her remarkable efforts and determination will become clear only after her planned retirement in several years. Moreover, those teachers who have rallied around a common cause to help homeless children and their families will one day leave B. F. Day. Will their replacements continue to understand and respond to the cry of a new group of disheartened mothers and children caught in the plight of poverty? Will the nostalgic reminiscence of the early days at B. F. Day sustain mothers like Debbie, Ronda, Lena, and Barbara long after their children have moved on to the middle school and beyond? Above all, when those students currently reaping the benefits of KOOL-IS find themselves facing two roads that diverge in a wood, how many will follow the one less traveled and find their way to a better life?

These are only some of the questions that await investigation through the course of future research. As with many stories, this is only the beginning. Recently, through the Seattle school district's Effective Schools Initiative for Homeless Youth, five public schools were mandated to adopt the KOOL-IS model upon bureaucratic acknowledgment of its success at B. F. Day. This occurrence provides an immediate opportunity to study whether a grass-roots program such as KOOL-IS is likely to function equally well in neighboring schools. The question of "generalizability" can be answered over time, as the hypotheses that are valid within the local context that spawned them do or do not hold up as well in other contexts.

One must acknowledge, however, that the needs of each school and each neighborhood differ. Guba and Lincoln (1988) have reminded us that "whether or not certain information is generalizable is a function not only of the degree to which the locale of the study is in fact a 'slice of life' but also of whether that particular 'slice of life' is representative of other 'slices of life'" (p. 116). In this way, they have suggested, the idea of "generalizability" is supplanted by the idea of "fittingness." It remains for the reader to make his or her own informed judgment as to degree of "fittingness" of program characteristics based on the facts presented herein, if transfer of this model is contemplated.

Finally, the professional growth of those teachers who played a vital role in the launching of KOOL-IS and of those yet to come suggests the need for further research in an area I will refer to as "empathic communication skills." We need to help all teachers build a sincere and compassionate understanding of the everyday life struggle many of their students face. For teachers, like all people, must come to terms with their own fear, prejudice, and confusion if they are to teach effectively and work alongside socially and economically impoverished children and parents.

School has traditionally been a place where children are asked and expected to change their thinking and their behavior between the hours of 9:00 and 3:00. Goodlad (1984) highlights "this strangely unique characteristic of classroom life":

> [There exists] the not quite successful but extraordinarily persistent pretense that human existence can be segmented, that part of it can be left outside the classroom door. The whole comes together again in the hallways, on the playground, and off the school site. But to bring the whole person into the classroom and to attempt to deal with him or her there, in large numbers, is to threaten the very existence of this partial ecosystem. (p. 243)

This truthful portrait of school life underscores the basic assumption upon which educational institutions across the nation generally function; that is, it is the child's nature, character, outlook on life, and behavior that must change to fit the school. One of the most intriguing questions relevant to educational change has been posed by Bowles and Gintis (1976) in their widely acclaimed book, *Schooling in Capitalist America*. In their inspirational and challenging text, the authors have asked, "Why in a democratic society, should an individual's first real contact with a formal institution be so profoundly antidemocratic?" To be sure, students are more often than not overlooked as individuals whose opinions matter. Conformity, subordination, and a kind of assumed acquiescence are expected, imposed, and rewarded by teachers and administrators. Viewed as the recipients of educational practice, change, or reform, children are rarely given the opportunity to influence decisions regarding what they learn, how they learn, or when they learn it.

Increasingly alienated from the hierarchical establishment of school rules, regulations, and requirements—as well as from the selection and determination of what is to be taught within the social environment in which they spend six waking hours a day—students frequently demonstrate a resistance toward or subversion of authoritarian rule. Their display of negative power, while elicited by a heightened sense of feeling objectified, inanimate, and helpless, is often misunderstood and only adds to the climate of alienation between teacher and student (Barth, 1990; Comer, 1980; Goodlad, 1984; Sizer, 1985). Lawton, Leithwood, Batcher, Donaldson, and Stewart (1988) have stated:

> Research on school related factors has focused largely on student behaviors in school on the implicit assumption that it is the student who must change to fit the school. Hence, interventions to reduce dropout rates often take the form of counselling and the like. [But future interventions] ought to assume that it is the school rather than or in addition to the student which needs to change. (p. 27)

VOICES IN THE COMMUNITY

Numerous articles in the *Seattle Times* in the fall of 1990 attracted public attention to the KOOL-IS program. Reaction was mixed; for example, store owners in the school's neighborhood held opinions about KOOL-IS that ranged from rejection through unconcern to acceptance. One gentleman forcefully stated, "The school has no business playing the role of mother, father, and banker. That's not what I pay my taxes for. Let the schools educate the kids, and let the government worry about the rest." However, another said, "I don't care what the schools do as long as kids stop dealing drugs outside my door in broad daylight." And, of course, there were those voices in the community that were lifted in praise.

Among the latter were those of the parishioners of the Mercer Island United Methodist Church who had become involved with the school's efforts. During my stay in Seattle, I invited several of them to my hotel room for coffee and conversation. I placed a tape recorder in the center of the table and asked that each person honestly and openly express his or her views regarding the role of the school as both a social service and educational agency. Taken together, their responses comprise a ringing endorsement of the reconstructionist viewpoint.

Bill Euster, a former teacher and current executive who has assumed an active role in arranging day care for the children of homeless but working mothers, asserted the following views:

> The question of who is responsible for the well-being of small children is the very question that gets us into trouble in the first place. As soon as some person says the schools are responsible, there are now a thousand reasons why the schools can't do this. And once you say the family is responsible, well it doesn't take but ten seconds to tell you why that is impossible.
>
> I don't care about identifying which institution, whether social service, school, or church, should be responsible. I believe that it is the cumulative effect of many individuals who care that becomes the solution. Every school has to have people that care within a small, geographically spaced pocket. We must think in terms of little neighborhoods and special communities within schools rather than city and state mandates which float in from distant, unconnected lands....
>
> Each school understands its own social fabric best. Accepting the fact that the surrounding community is layered in circles, each school must find ways to penetrate the maze and connect resources. I believe this is the essence of B. F. Day as I have come to understand it.

Leo Anderson, a retired attorney, picks up and delivers used furniture to those families who have been provided with affordable housing through the efforts of B. F. Day. He commented:

> People often say that it isn't the school's job to assume responsibility for the needs of impoverished children. They all too quickly say that it is society's job. To speak of society doing anything is a very generalized, meaningless statement. What do we mean when we say it is up to the society in which we live to take care of these problems? Who is "society" if it is not you and me? ...
>
> If it is at all possible for one school at a time to restructure its organization so it may effectively change the lives of those impoverished children in attendance, then it must do so. Not only because the school is ideally suited for such a task, but because the school is our only hope for the betterment of the human condition as we know it to be in the urban ghetto.

Pastor Jack Olive strongly proclaims a social reconstructionist view of education:

The question of whether schools will lose sight of their role as educational institutions should they begin to render social services is a question more often asked by "those who have" rather than by "those who have not."

Those of us "who have" are often concerned with sharing our human and monetary resources equally; if we put all our energy into caring for the children of the poor, we fear it will have a negative effect on the academic gains of our own children. However, if you ask those of us "who have" why our children are successful, our response suggests it is because of a stable home environment. If, in fact, this is the case, then it should not matter how much we invest in the concept of schooling as a response to unstable home lives.

By and large, the question of whether schools should assume the role of both a social and educational agency is a question which "the haves" ask and "the have nots" are not permitted to ask. I believe those of us "who have" need to share our resources, time, and energy because *all* children are equally deserving of that which we as parents want for our own children....

The school must stand in the vanguard of social change. Of this, I am sure. Addressing any and all social service issues needs to be a community effort; the school is simply the place where it happens because this is the common ground where all our children are gathered.

Joseph Johnson, Jr. (1992), Texas's first State Coordinator for the Education of Homeless Children, has commented:

> As America's public schools confront an increasing population of homeless students who present increasingly complex needs, schools have a choice. On the one hand, school staff can contend that they cannot or should not expand their services to address the needs of homeless children and youth. Perhaps other social service agencies should assume these responsibilities. Perhaps parents should be expected to do more. Perhaps the resources simply are insufficient. Perhaps the school cannot handle any more responsibilities. On the other hand, school staff can contend that they truly can make a difference. Perhaps the resources can be found. Perhaps it is primarily a change in attitude that is required. Perhaps school staff can insure that today's homeless children will not be tomorrow's homeless parents. Perhaps there truly is not a choice. (p. 175)

WHAT IF ... ?

I would like, for a moment, to suspend all scholarly and practical skepticism, and envision a course of research premised on the accomplishments at B. F. Day. The work at this one site—now expanding to encompass many of the schools in the state of Washington—is rich with implications for the future of all our schools and for the increasing proportion of at-risk children they serve.

Suppose for a moment that future researchers designate "trial sites" where an understanding of the social and economic realities of decaying family and community life, and their influence upon childhood development, is a critical and required part of the professional knowledge base of those teachers volunteering to serve at these sites. Suppose that there are many psychologists, family support workers, and case managers who work at these school sites and whose job it is to "connect" with children and families to determine the extent of unmet physical and psychological needs.

Suppose that organizational compartments and specializations are supplanted with community volunteers from all walks of life who are mobilized around a common cause: building and supporting the rock-bottom footholds essential for each and every student's escape from concentrated poverty, social dislocation, and psychological defeat.

Suppose that parents are an integral part of school life. Some are actually employed at the school, while others volunteer their time. Generative and sustained open discourse between parent and teacher greatly decreases the possibility of estrangement between home and school and in this way minimizes the need for parent or child to exercise their veto power—"the power not to learn, not to attend, not to behave well" (Comer, 1980, p. 27).

Imagine that "trial site" school life provides all of the everyday interactions, dilemmas, and conflicts that confront all of us in the world at large, and suppose that teachers teach strategies of conflict resolution and techniques to cope with those frustrations, delays in reward, and social rules of conduct by which we must abide in a civilized society. Unlike regular schools, cognitive and academic goals never take precedence over personal and social development; children learn to work and live in collaborative harmony with fellow students and significant adults. Children's absorption of democratic values and modes of creating and adapting harmonious group life within and beyond the walls of the schoolhouse assume focus and priority over intellectual and academic pursuits.

Imagine that teachers find ways of incorporating "open dialogue time" on a regular basis so that all students have an opportunity to become part of the decision-making process and in so doing become vocal and visible implementers of democratic modes of interaction. Students are a vital part of a just and fair system in which there is opportunity to voice opinions regarding the realistic "implementability" of cognitive and academic goals. In this way, children see the relevance of schooling in relation to the rest of their lives. The intrinsic motivation and desire to cooperate, share, participate, learn, and work toward experiences of individual as well as collective fulfillment are fostered because students feel that they belong and are a special part of the school. When the students commit to carrying out their role, their responsibilities, and their relevant and valued part within the context of school life, the onus for maintaining acceptable codes of behavior shifts from the teachers to the students. With the support of a significant adult, the child learns to tolerate frustration and disappointment and control disruptive impulses when pressures become too great. In addressing the developmental and personal needs of children, the "trial site" school creates a psychological sense of community and human well-being.

With the support and nurturance of a significant adult, children become empowered as they assume responsibility for their own words and actions and begin to see that behavior is actually an independent choice and within one's own control. Opportunities to make consistent connections between cause and effect within a nonjudgmental atmosphere foster trust and a desire to please.

Just suppose that future researchers and educators designed and studied such "trial site" schools. Quite apart from its potential value to the individuals involved, such an experiment in schooling could have incalculable value for educational research and reform. Even should the trial sites fail miserably—an unlikely outcome, in my view—the information gleaned in the effort would be of crucial import to future reform efforts.

The pressing contemporary social problems of poverty, joblessness, homelessness, urban decay, crime, and substance abuse have sown a great many seeds of disillusionment across the landscape of America. In many ways, we have lost faith in ourselves and in our most important social institution—our schools. Many of us have lost sight of the relevance of schooling to the rest of our lives. As we move into the twenty-first century, we must reconsider traditional, outdated concepts of education that no longer serve the needs of our children and families in a contemporary society suffering from moral, religious, and family ill health. The self-renewal of our society greatly depends on the vigorous restructuring of schools from bureaucracies into influential, collaborative networks offering a rebirth of hope, vision, and unity.

APPENDIX A

A Note to the Reader About Methodology

This qualitative case study is a sociohistorical narrative of why and how an urban public elementary school and its surrounding neighborhood collaborated in a unique program to assist homeless children and their families. The school's transformation into both a social and educational service agency is presented against the backdrop of social reconstructionist theory and the contemporary human conditions of poverty, hunger, and homelessness.

It is crucial to acknowledge very early on in any study the impossibility of eliminating unconscious as well as conscious bias in the perception of "favorable outcomes." To this end, precautions and procedures have been built into this study from its very inception to ensure neutrality of reported findings and to gauge the extent to which that neutrality has been achieved.

Different perspectives and attitudes held by all the major actors in this case study have been represented by the active voice of participants in direct and lengthy quotes. Readers will notice that some voices have been rendered in dialect and others have been rendered in standard English, despite the fact that each person's speech fell in different places on the continuums of pronunciation and grammar. The threshold between standard and nonstandard was inside my own ear. In this book, moreover, all these quotes have received the benefit of editing out repetitions, so that the reader can sense the cogency and forcefulness each interviewee conveyed in person. The fact that these independent stories and judgments tend to move in one direction, increases the likelihood that this case study has maintained standards of objectivity—in spite of my acknowledged bias, as described in the Preface. As Guba and Lincoln (1988) have noted, "When various bits of evidence all tend in one direction, that direction assumes far greater credibility" (p. 107).

Multiple sources of data were used, including systematic interviewing, direct observation, and study of pertinent documentation. A "snowball sample" was the primary source of interviewees. In February 1991, initial interviews began, starting with the principal, four faculty members, and several members of the community. The interviews at this stage of the study were accomplished by telephone, to overcome the distance between Seattle and my home in New York; they yielded 74 hours of recorded phone conversations. This first group of interviewees identified the second group: five teachers, seven community members, four case managers, two social workers, three clergymen, the head of the child study team affiliated with the University of Washington, and the external consultants who assisted in the transformation of the school.

In September 1991, during seven days of naturalistic observation, I was able to make face-to-face contact with these program participants, including nine parents and nine students who had no telephones. I also was able to make site visits to observe ongoing activities and to visit three of these students and their families, who had previously been homeless but were now living in residences obtained through the efforts of the B. F. Day network. In this way, all sides of the story—obtained from both skeptics and supporters—were appropriately documented.

In addition, over the three years between the conclusion of the initial research and the publication of this book, I have had hundreds of hours of telephone conversations and exchanged dozens of letters and faxes with program participants.

As a result of the on-site interviews, I have been able in many instances to meld descriptions of the setting itself with representative quotes from school and community participants about their perceptions of the school and neighborhood setting.

I used a question outline (see Appendix B) to make sure all areas of interest were covered in each interview. In addition, I established a high degree of rapport through unstructured conversations that effectively encouraged individuals to express ideas, feelings, and experiences in "their own language." The transcriptions of the tape recordings contain unabridged, verbatim accounts, edited only for repetition. In this way, it has been possible to extract and capture patterns, trends, themes, and nuances from various units of information.

To recount the process by which (1) school and family connections were slowly but surely forged and (2) participating individuals coalesced and persevered during the early stages of change at B. F. Day, I have presented illustrative experiences that appear to have affected the cognitions, emotions, and actions of the people directly involved. I also present the findings from my review of hundreds of program records and documents such as proposals for grants, financial and budget records, correspondence to and from outside social service agencies, routine records or intake sheets on students, organizational rules and regulations, and all other memoranda generated by or for the program.

Construct validity is of concern in this particular study since the focus is on how a school changed its character. In order to identify the critical, operational events that constitute this "change," the preexisting school climate is given as much attention as is the atmosphere in the school following the implementation of specified program components.

I employed three methods to establish internal validity or credibility in the study: (1) triangulation and corrobation using data collected from interviews, observations, and documentation; (2) host verification or "member checks," in which I verified my factual data with the people who had provided them; and (3) "phenomenon recognition," in which I presented my sense of "reality" at B. F. Day to those who live it so that they could verify the accuracy of my perceptions (Guba & Lincoln, 1988). In order to ensure internal reliability, I stayed alert to the possibility that I might misinterpret, oversimplify, or selectively filter information.

Finally, the recollections of individuals involved in any collective endeavor will tend to vary over time. The greater the number of people involved, the more complicated it is to get each element of the story to be "true." Goodlad (1984) has said: "Studying all of a school at once is virtually impossible. One inevitably looks at pieces and then seeks to put them together. The results are neither fully satisfying nor completely accurate. They are an approximation of reality—and then only one's own approximation." (p. 16)

It is my hope that I have been mindful enough of all these cautions and diligent enough in my research to have painted an accurate and evocative picture of B. F. Day, for what has been accomplished at this school should surely become a beacon that lights a way for us all.

APPENDIX B

RESEARCH QUESTIONS AND INTERVIEW PROTOCOLS

What objectives, activities, and events comprise KOOL-IS? Who are the people engaged in this network of interacting links?
(Interview Subjects: Principal, Faculty, Case Manager)

1. If you were describing KOOL-IS to someone who had never heard about it before, what would you tell them about it?
2. If I wanted to get a real "insider's view" of KOOL-IS, what aspects or services of the program should I focus on first?
3. Are there specific educational features to this program that differ from those rendered in the school as a whole?
4. Have modifications in the overall learning environment at B. F. Day accompanied the implementation of KOOL-IS? Give me an example of any modifications that have been implemented.
5. Are the educational features of this program applicable to all students or only to those students identified as homeless?
6. Describe this program in relation to its "place in the school." Are the features of this program implemented in all classrooms in which homeless students are in attendance, or are specific learning environments established and isolated for homeless students only?
7. How was initial funding obtained for the development of the program? Are there specific agencies, groups, or individuals who provide the necessary monetary and human resources required for the continued implementation of KOOL-IS?

8. How are the basic needs of homeless students assessed? How many people are involved in this assessment and who are they?
9. Are there specific lists of responsibilities or duties that are assigned to key people such as the teacher, case manager, nurse, transition room manager, and so forth?
10. From beginning to end, what is entailed in the initial welcome, registration, and placement of a homeless student?
11. What are the presumed direct benefits of this program once a child becomes an active member of KOOL-IS?
12. What features or components of the program are actually located at the school site?
13. Tell me about the "transition room." How does it differ from rooms of a similar nature in other schools?
14. What type of outreach features occur beyond school boundaries?
15. How is contact initiated with outside social service agencies?
16. How is information disseminated to the parents of students?
17. From beginning to end, what is entailed in the location of permanent housing?
18. Once a permanent residence is located, who and what are involved in the actual move of the family?
19. Who provides the funds, facilities, household furnishings, and physical movers needed in order to "set up a new home"?
20. In what ways are neighborhood people organized to form a network of interacting and resourceful links?

Why did Benjamin Franklin Day change from a previous state, as solely an educational agency, to a new state, as both a social and educational service agency? (Interview Subjects: Principal, Faculty)

1. How would you depict the school climate at B. F. Day prior to the decision to adopt the KOOL-IS model?
2. Describe a typical day at your school or in your class prior to the adoption of KOOL-IS, and describe how it reflects some of the social and academic challenges confronting homeless students and their teachers at that time. Contrast your recollection with the present situation on a typical day.
3. What were your thoughts or feelings regarding the situation at B. F. Day as you perceived it at that time?
4. Was there something specific about the school climate or the social and academic situation at B. F. Day that would explain why the principal and faculty changed the school's role?

5. Why did the school assume responsibility for the numerous social services rendered under this plan, rather than simply referring problems outside the academic domain to supplemental social service agencies?

6. Was there one specific social or academic challenge confronting homeless students and their teachers that might be considered the foremost reason B. F. Day assumed a position of change as depicted by the KOOL-IS model?

7. How did you view your role in dealing with the challenges presented by homeless students prior to KOOL-IS? How do you view your role now?

8. How do you think the other teachers/children in the school/ class felt about the homeless students attending B. F. Day?

9. How would you characterize the relationship between homeless and nonhomeless students prior to KOOL-IS? Do you perceive the situation differently now?

10. How would you describe the ways in which homeless students felt about themselves and their situation at B. F. Day?

11. Were there any unusual episodes involving a homeless child that stand out in your mind?

12. What do you recall as being the most challenging aspect in working with homeless students prior to "KOOL-IS? How did you deal with this challenge at that time? How are things now?

13. Prior to adoption of the KOOL-IS model, did you feel you should be responsible for the education and well-being of homeless kids?

14. Who did you think should assume responsibility for the food, clothing, shelter, and medical and psychological care of such children? Why?

15. Overall, how would you describe the role played by this school in community affairs prior to KOOL-IS? How do you perceive the school's role in community affairs now?

16. At that time, did you have personal feelings about the homeless situation in the surrounding community and the role the school should or should not assume?

17. Prior to KOOL-IS, how did you experience the relationship between teacher and parent or school and family? And now?

18. How do you personally experience some of the specific aspects of KOOL-IS (providing clothes, shelter, self-esteem, hope), and what do they mean to you?

19. Personally, did you agree with the claims made for the program? What good did you believe was likely to come of it? What bad effects did you think it might have?

20. Have you experienced changes in your own feelings about home-less children since the implementation of the program? Describe these changes.

21. Can you draw an analogy between KOOL-IS and any other experi-ence you have had insofar as what the program "looks like and feels like to you"?

22. In what ways does the program take you out of the classroom both physically and psychologically? Do you feel less isolated, more col-legial, different? In what ways?

23. Elaborate on some of the thoughts you have concerning this pro-gram's operations, outcomes, strengths and weaknesses.

24. What features of the KOOL-IS model do you believe to be most salient to teachers, students, and parents?

25. What types of changes have you perceived in yourself as a result of your involvement in this program (feelings about self, attitudes toward work, aspirations, satisfactions)?

26. Knowing what you now know, do you believe the school made the appropriate decision in assuming responsibility for the numerous social services rendered under this plan? Should the school have simply referred problems outside the academic domain to supple-mental social service agencies?

How did the school transform itself into both a social and educational service agency? What prompted individuals to coalesce and persevere as a network? (Interview Subjects: Princi-pal, Faculty, Consultants)

1. Who conceptualized (designed, planned, developed) KOOL-IS?

2. Who identified the local need to which this program is purport-edly a response?

3. Was the need identified through a formal process (context evaluation of school and community composition) or through an informal pro-cess (determination made by principal or teachers based on perceived circumstances at the time)?

4. What types of situations or circumstances led you to perceive the need for some kind of change within the school itself?

5. Who initiated the idea of applying the KOOL-IS model to meet the needs of school and community?

6. Was there a local social service agency involved in this decision apart from the school?

7. How was the idea of KOOL-IS presented to the school staff?

8. What was the staff's initial response, and how did that response change over time?

9. How was the ideology underlying this program presented to the broader community? What was the community's initial response?

10. Were there individuals or groups who perceived negative side effects resulting from KOOL-IS?

11. Are you aware of any conflicts that emerged between people who had strong feelings about this program, pro or con?

12. Were there staff development or in-service training classes that focused primarily on homeless children, their families, and the challenges that confront them?

13. Did these sessions affect or change your perceptions or feelings about homeless students and the ways in which one might relate to them in the classroom situation?

14. Did you ever consider leaving the program at the time of initial inception or during the early phase of implementation?

15. Were there specific experiences or events that prompted you to coalesce and persevere as part of a collaborative network?

16. Give an example of how individual team members were encouraged to express and set their own goals.

17. Is there a particular staff development meeting that you can tell me about in detail?

18. Could you prioritize factors that enhanced sharing of feelings and a sense of trust in other team members?

19. Were there incidents when you could not arrive at mutually acceptable solutions? In such cases, how was conflict managed effectively? How was the group encouraged to persevere toward a course of action?

20. Describe one incident in which one team member saw another's point of view and clearly articulated that view in a conflict situation, thereby enhancing clarity.

21. What types of procedures were developed and implemented for evaluating both the process and outcome of KOOL-IS?

22. Give me an example of a particular intervention procedure that was designed to remediate weaknesses in the program.

23. In what ways did the principal actively engage in the implementation of KOOL-IS? (a) attended meetings, (b) positive attention to staff, (c) frequent classroom visits, (d) award system.

24. In what ways was the purpose of schooling as conceived by the principal communicated to the faculty and students?

25. At any time, did the principal articulate a "vision of the school" that headed everyone in the same direction?

26. Can you describe the ways in which the principal's "vision" was translated into programs and activities within the school?
27. Did the adoption of KOOL-IS affect the educational goals, expectations, and programs delineated by the principal prior to the creation of KOOL-IS? Do you perceive the effect as positive or negative in regard to educational outcomes?
28. Identify some of the ways in which external consultant evaluation assistance was helpful.
29. How were neighborhood people organized to form a network of interacting and resourceful links? How were local businesses and social service agencies encouraged to become part of the KOOL-IS program?
30. Could you prioritize those factors (parent/teacher contact, local neighborhood efforts, advocacy of the principal) that enhance the desired outcomes resulting from KOOL-IS?

Proposed interview questions for students and parents (Interview Subjects: Students and Parents)

1. If you were describing KOOL-IS to someone who had never heard about it before, what would you tell that person?
2. How did you first learn about the KOOL-IS program?
3. What thoughts went through your mind at that time?
4. What were your feelings about the homeless situation and the role the school should or should not assume?
5. Prior to KOOL-IS, how would you describe the ways in which homeless students felt about themselves and their situation at Benjamin Franklin Day Elementary School?
6. Describe an average day at B. F. Day before the KOOL-IS program came about. Describe an average school day now.
7. What was the relationship between homeless students and their teachers? Between homeless and nonhomeless students?
8. Did parents feel comfortable going into the school building to see their child's teacher? How do parents feel about it now?
9. What were your feelings about the education homeless children were receiving at their school? What is your feeling now?
10. Were there any unusual episodes involving a homeless student that stand out in your mind?
11. Prior to KOOL-IS, how did you feel about your (child's) educational experience on a daily basis? What was your (child's) attendance like?

12. What educational or social features of the KOOL-IS model do you believe to be the most important?
13. How do you personally experience some of the specific aspects of KOOL-IS (clothes, shelter, food, self-esteem, hope) and what do they mean to you?
14. In what ways does the program help you with the crises that you must face on a daily basis?
15. Do you know of individuals who perceive negative side effects resulting from KOOL-IS?
16. How would you describe life in school now? Is your (child's) educational experience better? Is it easier to relate to teachers and other students? Has your (child's) attendance improved?
17. Has KOOL-IS changed your views and hopes for the future?

References

Addams, J. (1910). *Twenty years at Hull House.* New York: Macmillan.

Ahola-Sidaway, J. A. (1988, April). *From Gemeinschaft to Gesellschaft: A case study of student transition from elementary school to high school.* Paper presented at the annual meeting of the American Education Research Association, New Orleans.

Allington, R. [1991]. Effective literacy instruction for at-risk children. In M. Knapp & P. Shields (Eds.), *Better schooling for the children of poverty: Alternatives to conventional wisdom* (pp. 9–30). Berkeley, CA: McCutchan.

Allington, R., & McGill-Franzen, A. (1989). Different programs, indifferent instruction. In D. Lipsky & A. Gartner (Eds.), *Beyond separate education* (pp.75–94). Baltimore: Brookes.

Andrews, R. (1988). *Illinois principal as institutional leader* (Report to the Illinois Association of School Principals). Springfield, IL.

Andrews, R., Soder, R., & Jacoby, D. (1986, April). *Principal roles, student achievement, and the other school variables.* Paper presented at the annual meeting of the American Education Research Association, San Francisco.

Angelos, C. (1989, May 20). Youth advocate fasts for children. *Seattle Times,* p. a12.

Applebee, A., Langer, J., & Mullis, I. (1988). *Who reads best?* Princeton, NJ: Educational Testing Service.

Ascher, C. (1988, March). *Improving the school–home connection for low-income urban parents.* (Digest: ERIC/CUE No. 41, ED 293973).

Ashton, P., & Webb, R. (1986). *Making a difference: Teachers' sense of efficacy and student achievement.* New York: Longman.

Barth, R. (1990). *Improving schools from within: Teachers, parents and principals can make the difference.* San Francisco: Jossey-Bass.

Bassuk, E., & Gallagher, E. (1990). No fixed address: The effects of homelessness on families and children. *Child and Youth Services, 14,* 35–47.

Bennis, W. (1986). Transformative power and leadership. In T. Sergiovanni, *Leadership and organizational culture* (pp. 64–71). Chicago: University of Illinois Press.

Berman, P., & McLaughlin, M. (1977). *Federal programs supporting educational change: Vol. VII. Factors affecting implementation and continuation.* Santa Monica, CA: Rand Corporation.

Berman, P., McLaughlin, M., Pincus, J., Weiler, D., & Williams, R. (1979). *An exploratory study of school district adaptations.* Santa Monica, CA: Rand Corporation.

Block, P. (1987). *The empowered manager.* San Francisco, CA: Jossey-Bass.

Blumberg, A., & Greenfield, W. (1981). *The effective principal.* Boston: Allyn & Bacon.

Bowles, S., & Gintis, H. (1976). *Schooling in capitalist America.* New York: Basic Books.

Broikou, K., Allington, R., & Jachym, N. (1989). The impact of the Felton decision in one archdiocese. *Remedial and Special Education, 10,* 29–34.

Brophy, J. (1991). Effective schooling for disadvantaged students. In M. Knapp & P. Shields (Eds.), *Better schooling for the children of poverty: Alternatives to conventional wisdom* (pp. 211–234). Berkeley, CA: McCutchan.

Center for Law and Education. (1990). *Educating homeless children and youth: a sample of programs, policies and procedures.* Cambridge, MA: Author.

Children's Defense Fund. (1991). *The state of America's children.* Washington, DC: Author.

Clark, D., & Meloy, J. (1990). Recanting bureaucracy: A democratic structure for leadership in schools. In A. Lieberman (Ed.), *Schools as collaborative cultures: Creating the future now* (pp. 3–23). New York: Falmer.

Cohen, M. (1988). Designing state assessment systems. *Phi Delta Kappan, 70*(8), 583–588.

Comer, J. (1980). *School power.* New York: Free Press.

Comer, J. (1988, January). Is "parenting" essential to good teaching? *Families and Schools,* pp. 34–39.

Cooper, M. (1988). Whose culture is it, anyway? In A. Lieberman (Ed.), *Building a professional culture in schools* (pp. 45–54). New York: Teachers College Press.

Crandall, D., Eiseman, J., & Louis, K. (1986). Strategic planning issues that bear on the success of school improvement efforts. *Educational Administration Quarterly, 22*(3), 21–53.

Cremin, L. (1988). *American education.* New York: Harper & Row.

Cuban, L. (1988). A fundamental puzzle of school reform. *Phi Delta Kappan, 70*(5), 341–344.

Darling-Hammond, L. (1990). Teacher professionalism: Why and how. In A. Lieberman (Ed.), *Schools as collaborative cultures: Creating the future now* (pp. 25–50). New York: Falmer.

Dauber, S., & Epstein, J. (1993). Parents' attitudes and practices of involvement in inner-city elementary and middle schools. In N. Chavkin (Ed.), *Families and schools in a pluralistic society* (pp. 53–71). Albany: SUNY Press.

Deci, E. (1976). The hidden costs of rewards. *Organizational Dynamics, 4*(3), 61–72.

Dewey, J. (1899). *The school and society.* Chicago: University of Chicago Press.

Doll, R. (1989). *Curriculum improvements.* Boston: Allyn & Bacon.

Dossey, J., Mullis, V., Lindquist, M., & Chambers, D. (1988). *The mathematics report card: Are we measuring up?* Princeton, NJ: Educational Testing Service.

Eisner, E., & Vallance, E. (1974). *Conflicting conceptions of curriculum.* Berkeley, CA: McCutchan.

Epstein, J. (1991). Effects on student achievement of teachers' practices for parent involvement. In S. Silvern (Ed.), *Literacy through family, community, and school interaction* (pp. 261–276). Greenwich, CT: JAI Press.

Etzioni, A. (1988). *The moral dimension toward a new economics.* New York: Free Press.

Farr Whiteman, M. (Ed.) (1980). *Reactions to Ann Arbor: Vernacular black English and education.* Washington, DC: Center for Applied Linguistics.

Fine, M. (1993). [Ap]parent involvement: Reflections on parents, power and urban public schools. *Teachers College Record, 94*(4), 682–710.

Firestone, W. (1989). Using reform: Conceptualizing district initiatives. *Educational evaluation and policy analysis, 11*(2), 151–164.

Firestone, W., & Rosenblum, S. (1988). *The alienation and commitment of students and teachers in urban high schools.* Washington, DC: Rutgers University and Office of Educational Research and Improvement.

Frake, C. (1977). Plying frames can be dangerous: Some reflections on methodology in cognitive anthropology. *Quarterly Newsletter of the Institute for Comparative Human Development, 1*(3), 1–7.

Fullan, M. (1982). *The meaning of educational change.* New York: Teachers College Press.

Fullan, M. (1991). *The new meaning of educational change.* New York: Teachers College Press.

Fullan, M., & Park, P. (1981). *Curriculum implementation: A resource booklet.* Toronto: Ontario Ministry of Education.

Garcia, G., Jimenez, R., & Pearson, P. (1989). *An annotated bibliography of research related to the reading of at-risk children* (Tech. Rep. No. 482). Urbana-Champaign: University of Illinois, Center for the Study of Reading.

Garman, N. (1982). The clinical approach to supervision. In T. Sergiovanni (Ed.), *Supervision of teaching* (pp. 35–52). Alexandria, VA: Association for Supervision and Curriculum Development.

Good, T., & Biddle, B. (1988). Research and the improvement of mathematics instruction: The need for observational resources. In D. Grouws & T. Cooney (Eds.), *Perspectives on research on effective mathematics teaching.* Reston, VA: National Council of Teachers of Mathematics.

Goodlad, J. (1979). *What schools are for.* Bloomington, IN: Phi Delta Kappa Educational Foundation.

Goodlad, J. (1984). *A place called school.* New York: McGraw-Hill.

Goodlad, J. (1987). *The ecology of school renewal.* Chicago: University of Chicago Press.

Goodman, L., & Lieberman, A. (1985, April). *Effective assister behavior: What they brought and what they learned.* Paper presented at the annual meeting of the American Educational Research Association, Chicago.

Goodman, Y. M., Watson, D. J., & Burke, C. L. (1987). *Reading miscue inventory.* New York: Richard C. Owen.

Grannis, J. (1967). The school as a model of society. *Harvard Graduate School of Education Alumni Association Bulletin, 12,* 14–27.

Grant, C. (1989). Equity, equality, teachers, and classroom life. In W. Secada (Ed.), *Equity in education* (pp. 89–102). Philadelphia, PA: Falmer.

Griffin, G. (1988). Leadership for curriculum improvement: The school administrator's role. In A. Lieberman (Ed.), *Schools as collaborative cultures: Creating the future now* (pp. 195–211). New York: Falmer.

Guba, E., & Lincoln, Y. (1988). *Effective evaluation.* London: Jossey-Bass.

Hagen, J., & Ivanoff, A. (1988). Homeless women: A high-risk population. *Affilia, 3*(1), 19–33.

Hall, G., & Griffin, T. (1980, April). *Implementation at the school building level: The development and analysis of nine mini-case studies.* Papers presented at the annual meeting of the American Educational Research Association, Boston. (ERIC No. 207170).

Hall, G., & Loucks, S. (1977). A developmental model for determining whether the treatment is actually implemented. *American Education Research Journal, 14*(3), 263–276.

Hall, J., & Maza, P. (1990). No fixed address: The effects of homelessness on families and children. *Child and Youth Services, 14,* 35–47.

Hargreaves, A. (1989). *Curriculum and assessment reform.* London: Open University Press.

Haynes, M., & Jenkins, J. (1986). Reading instruction in special education resource rooms. *American Educational Research Journal, 23,* 161–190.

Homewords. (1991, March). [Quarterly publication of the Homelessness Information Exchange, Washington, DC], *3* (1).

Huberman, M., & Miles, M. (1986). Rethinking the quest for school improvement: Some findings from the DESSI study. In A. Lieberman (Ed.), *Rethinking school improvement* (pp. 61–81). New York: Teachers College Press.

Johnson, Jr., J. (1992). Educational support services for homeless children and youth. In J. Stronge (Ed.), *Educating homeless children and adolescents* (pp. 153–176). Newbury Park, CA: Sage.

King, A., Warren, W., & Peart, M. (1988). *The teaching experience.* Toronto: Ontario Secondary School Teachers' Federation.

Kozol, J. (1985). *The illiterate America.* New York: Anchor.

Lawton, S., Leithwood, K., Batcher, E., Donaldson, E., & Stewart, R. (1988). *Student retention and transition in Ontario high schools: Policies, practices, and prospects.* Toronto: Ministry of Education.

Lieberman, A., & Miller, L. (1986). School improvement: Themes and variations. In A. Lieberman (Ed.), *Rethinking school improvement* (pp. 96–111). New York: Teachers College Press.

Lieberman, A., & Miller, L. (1992). *Teachers: Their world and their work*. New York: Teachers College Press.

Little, J. (1982). Norms of collegiality and experimentation: workplace conditions of school success. *American Educational Research Journal, 19*, 325–340.

Little, J. W. (1987). Teachers as colleagues. In V. Richardson-Koehler (Ed.), *Educators' handbook: A research perspecitve* (pp. 491–510). New York: Falmer.

Lortie, D. (1975). *Schoolteacher: A sociological study*. Chicago: University of Chicago Press.

Louis, K., & Miles, M. (1990). *Improving the urban high school: What works and why*. New York: Teachers College Press.

Marris, P. (1975). *Loss and change*. New York: Anchor Press/Doubleday.

Marsh, D. (1988, April). *Key factors associated with the effective implementation and impact of California's educational reform*. Paper presented at the annual meeting of the American Educational Research Association, New Orleans.

Marsh, D., & Bowman, G. (1988). *State initiated top-down versus bottom-up reform in secondary school*. Madison: University of Wisconsin Press.

McDermott, R. (1987). The explanation of minority school failure, again. *Anthropology and Education Quarterly, 18*(4), 361–364.

McGill-Franzen, A., & Allington, R. (1990). Comprehension and coherence: Neglected elements of literacy instruction in remedial and resource room services. *Journal of Reading, Writing, and Learning Disabilities, 6*(2), 149–182.

McKinney Homeless Assistance Act. (July 22, 1987). Public Law no. 100-77. 101, Stat. 482, and the Amendments to this Act (November 7, 1988). Public Law no. 100-628. 102, Stat. 3224.

McLaughlin, M., & Pfeifer, R. (1988). *Teacher evaluation: Improvement, accountability, and effective learning*. New York: Teachers College Press.

McLaughlin, M., & Yee, S. (1988). School as a place to have a career. In A. Lieberman (Ed.), *Building a professional culture in schools* (pp. 23–44). New York: Teachers College Press.

Miles, M. (1987, April). *Practical guidelines for school administrators: How to get there*. Paper presented at the annual meeting of the American Educational Research Association, CITY.

Moll, L. C., Estrada, E., Diaz, E., & Lopes, L. M. (1980). The organization of bilingual lessons: Implications for schooling. *Quarterly Newsletter of the Laboratory of Comparative Human Cognition, 2*, 53–58.

Molnar, J. (1988). *Home is where the heart is: The crisis of homeless children and families in New York City* (Report to the Edna McConnell Clark Foundation). New York: Bank Street College of Education.

Moos, R. (1974). Systems for the assessment and classification of human environments. In R. H. Moos & P. M. Insel, *Issues in social ecology: Human milieus* (pp. 5–28). Palo Alto, CA: National Press Books.

Mortimore, P., Sammons, P., Stoll, L., Lewis, D., & Ecob, R. (1988). *School matters: The junior years*. London: Open Books.

National Association of State Coordinators for the Education of Homeless Children and Youth. (1992). *In the shadow of opportunity: Removing barriers and creating success for America's homeless children and youth.* Baltimore: Maryland State Department of Education.

National Center for Children in Poverty. (1990). *Five million children : A statistical profile of our poorest young citizens.* New York: Columbia University, School of Public Health.

National Coalition for the Homeless. (1990). *Newsletter.*

Natriello, G., McDill, E., & Pallas, A. (1990). *Schooling disadvantaged children: Racing against catastrophe.* New York: Teachers College Press.

Oakes, J. (1985). *Keeping track.* New Haven, CN: Yale University Press.

Passow, H. (1984). *Reforming schools in the 1980s: A critical review of the national reports.* Teachers College, Columbia University, New York. (Digest: ERIC/CUE, ED No. 242859)

Peters, W. (1971). *A class divided.* New York: Doubleday.

Peters, T. J., & Waterman, R. H. (1982). *In search of excellence: Lessons from America's best-run companies.* New York: Harper & Row.

Peterson, P. (1988). Teachers' and students' cognitional knowledge for classroom teaching and learning. *Educational Researcher, 17*(5), 5–14.

Proshansky, E., & Wolfe, M. (1975). The physical setting and open education. In T. G. David & B. D. Wright (Eds.), *Learning environments* (pp. 31–48). Chicago: University of Chicago Press.

Ravitch, D. (1985). *The schools we deserve.* New York: Basic Books.

Rist, R. (1970). Student social class and teacher expectation: The self-fulfilling prophecy in ghetto education. *Harvard Educational Review, 40,* 411–451.

Rosenholtz, S. (1986). *The organizational context of teaching* (Interim Report to NIE, Grant # NIE-G-83-0041). Washington, DC: National Institute of Education.

Rosenholtz, S. (1989). *Teachers'workplace: The social organization of schools.* New York: Longman.

Russell, S., & Friel, S. (1989, March). *Dimensions of reality in elementary math problems.* Paper presented at the annual meeting of the American Educational Research Association, San Francisco.

Rutter, M., Maugham, B., Mortimer, P., Ouston, J., & Smith, A. (1979). *Fifteen thousand hours: Secondary schools and their effects on children.* Cambridge, MA: Harvard University Press.

Sarason, S. (1977). *Human services and resource networks.* San Francisco: Jossey-Bass.

Sarason, S. (1982). *The culture of the school and the problem of change.* Boston: Allyn & Bacon.

Schlechty, P. (1990). *Schools for the twenty-first century.* San Francisco: Jossey-Bass.

Schorr, L. (1988). *Within our reach: Breaking the cycle of disadvantage.* New York: Doubleday.

Sergiovanni, T. (1984). Leadership as cultural expression. In T. Sergiovanni

& J. Corbally (Eds.), *Leadership and organizational culture* (pp. 105–114). Chicago: University of Illinois Press.

Sergiovanni, T. (1991). *The principalship.* Boston: Allyn & Bacon.

Sizer, T. (1985). *Horace's compromise: The dilemma of the American high school.* Boston: Houghton Mifflin.

Slavin, R. (Ed.) (1989). *School and classroom organization.* Hillsdale, NJ: Erlbaum.

Smith, W., & Andrews, R. (1989). *Instructional leadership: How principals make a difference.* Alexandria, VA: Association for Supervision and Curriculum Development.

Sommer, R. (1969). *Personal space.* Englewood Cliffs, NJ: Prentice-Hall.

Steele, F. (1973). *Physical settings and organizational development.* Redding, MA: Addison-Wesley.

Sykes, G. (1990). Teaching incentives: Constraint and variety. In A. Lieberman, *Schools as collaborative cultures: Creating the future now* (pp. 103–125). New York: Falmer.

Tobis, D. (1985). Services to children. In C. Brecher & R. Horton (Eds.), *Setting municipal priorities: 1986* (pp. 207–234). New York: New York University Press.

Tyack, D. (1974). *The one best system.* Cambridge, MA: Harvard University Press.

U.S. Department of Education. (1989). *Report to Congress on final reports submitted by states in accordance with Section 724 (b) (3) of the Stewart B. McKinney Homeless Assistance Act.* Washington, DC: Author.

van Ry, M. (1990). *Homeless families: Causes, effects, and recommendations.* Doctoral dissertation, University of Washington, Seattle. *Dissertation Abstracts International,* Abstract No. 01118966 (Order No. AAD 90-26030).

Ward, B., & Pascarelli, J. (1987). Networking for educational improvement. In J. Goodlad (Ed.), *The ecology of school renewal.* Chicago, IL: University of Chicago Press.

Wigginton, E. (1986). *Sometimes a shining moment: The Foxfire experience.* New York: Anchor.

Wilson, W. (1987). *The truly disadvantaged: The inner city, the underclass, and public policy.* Chicago: University of Chicago Press.

Wilson, W., & Corcoran, T. (1988). *Successful secondary schools: Visions of excellence in American public education.* Philadelphia: Falmer.

Wirt, F., & Kirst, M. (1992). *Schools in conflict.* Berkeley, CA: McCutchan.

Yee, S. (1987). *Teacher turnover: Career commitment and professional involvement.* Doctoral dissertation, Stanford University, Stanford, CA.

Ziegler, S. (1987). *The effects of parent involvement on children's achievement: The significance of home/school links.* Toronto: Toronto Board of Education: Research Section, Library Services Department.

Index

About the Author

SHARON QUINT GOTTLIEB, a learning disabilities specialist who maintains a private practice, holds an Ed.D. with a specialty in leadership (Columbia University, Teachers College), the certificate of administrative supervisor of education (Teachers College), and master's degrees in developmental psychology (Teachers College) and reading/learning disabilities (New York University). She has been a clinician in developmental psychology and reading/learning disabilities at Brooklyn Jewish Hospital, New York, working with children with special needs; she has taught special education classes at P.S. 225 in Brooklyn; she has been the educational evaluator of the Mount Vernon, New York, elementary and secondary school systems; and she is an active volunteer with homeless people in New York City. Dr. Quint lives in Westchester, New York, with her husband, Jay Gottlieb, and their children, Lauren, aged 14, and Ricky, aged 12.